20x20

KETO DIET

Cookbook

Lose 20 Pounds in 20 Days

Effortless Meal Plan

Megan Peterson

Warning-Disclaimer

The purpose of this book is to educate and entertain. The author or publisher does not guarantee that anyone following the techniques, suggestions, tips, ideas, or strategies will become successful. The author and publisher shall have neither liability or responsibility to anyone with respect to any loss or damage caused, or alleged to be caused, directly or indirectly by the information contained in this book.

Contents

CHAPTER 5: DINNER 57

CHAPTER 6: DESSERTS..84

THE 20-DAY MEAL PLAN TO LOSE 20 POUNDS 90

Introduction

Understanding the craze of the Ketogenic Diet

I'll tell you. Long before we got all "richly" about meals – I mean loading our plates with meats, cheeses, and creamy goodness; the folks dating back from 500 BC were already on this spree.

To them, they left carbohydrates out of their diets to treat epilepsy in children and ate foods with high fats,proteins, and many green vegetables. And guess what? It worked!

This is what the Ketogenic Diet is, removing high carbs from foods and eating high fats and proteins instead. It solves a diverse range of ailments by merely reducing the amounts of sugars in the body and allowing good fats play a healing role.

Usually, the body will "lazily" burn energy from carbohydrates because it is easiest while fats, which are supposed to be burned for energy, sit in the body and do nothing. Because they lay idle, your love handles keep increasing, your cheeks get plumper, and you find fats in all the areas of your body that you will rather prefer that they weren't.

Thanks to the many researchers that dug out this ancient secret, it is a diet for now and for the future. Having been embraced by many medical practitioners and healthy living enthusiasts, it is of no surprise that the Ketogenic Diet is one of the first recommendations for curing varying ailments – this is how far good craze has gone.

For me, it is a feel-good kind of a diet. It keeps me sane, light-weighted, and feeling fresh within and out; I couldn't ask for more.

Chapter 1: The Ketogenic Diet

The positives of the Ketogenic Diet

Blood Sugar Control

Starchy foods and sugary foods produce sugars in the body. This is why people with diabetes suffer, and to my surprise, in the past, meal plans created for people with diabetes were loaded with carbohydrates, fruits, and processed milk. So wrong!

By avoiding carbohydrates, the amount of sugars in the body drops drastically, which requires a relative reduction in the use of diabetic medication.

Significant enough, there are many testimonies of the Keto diet healing diabetics completely; that's some good news right there!

Weight loss

It goes without stressing that you're up for a significant weight shed once you start dieting the Keto way. Why so? Because your body now burns all the stored up fat in your body for energy.

Like I said earlier when on carbs, the body's duty to consume fats gets dormant and will rather burn carbs. But, when carbohydrates are reduced, the body is moved into a metabolic state called ketosis where it is forced to burn fats.

Appetite Control

Ever wondered why there is a word as "sweet-tooth"? The more sugars you eat, the more of it you will want. Therefore, the unexpected hunger pangs after taking sugary foods or fruits.

Appetite levels increase, not necessarily, because the body needs food. It is because the body burns sugars fast and creates a false alert that it needs more food.The truth is it just needs some SUGAR.

On the keto diet, fat burns slower keeping the body fuller for an extended period. I usually find myself eating twice a day on a healthy meal because my breakfast is fat-rich and keeps me full past my lunch period sometimes.

If hungry in between meals, I snack on a Keto option, and I'm good.

Energy Levels

Starch and sugars are tricky – they satisfy fast, but burn out fast. When this happens, the body is left weak and craves more carbs only to be burned quickly again. Energy levels then fluctuate causing most parts of the body to be less vibrant.

On the other hand, feeding on high fats and Proteins create a steady level of energy because fats and Protein burn gradually and in a consistent manner.

Keto Diet and Insulin Resistance

On a high carb diet, the body breaks starch into useful sugar components known as glucose, which is transported to the muscles and tissues as energy. The carrier of this glucose is insulin – meant to be a good thing.

However, in cases where the body becomes resistant to insulin, sugar breaks lose in the body. Once, the liver, cells in the muscles, and fats stop absorbing the sugars, they find their way into the blood and have a free flow – diabetes sets in.

Through the Keto diet, this problem is prevented because the body is naturally reduced of sugars through carb reduction hence there is more control over the amount of sugar needed in the body.

Why fats and Proteins – does this mean carbohydrates are bad?

No, don't get it twisted. Carbohydrates aren't bad for the sense that they are nature's gift for feeding. However, for their starchy and sugary components, a small measure of carb intake should be considered to avoid increased sugar levels and low energy.

Fats and Pproteins, on the other hand, are safer options to consume in larger quantities. They are a more sustainable way of providing energy to the body, lead to weight loss, and are entirely healthy to the body.

Meanwhile, fats can be categorized into two parts: good and bad fats. Below I give examples of some good fats, but mostly these are sourced from natural ingredients like meat, fatty fish, nuts, avocados, tofu, and seeds. While bad fats are often processed products, for example, some "vegetable oils."

Concisely, you want to ensure that you are deriving your fats from natural sources and using vegetables with low carb counts if you need to eat carbohydrates like rice.

Side effects of the Ketogenic Diet

While it sucks to say that the Keto Diet has its wrong sides, it sure does like every other thing.

Frequent urination

Which is a good thing! Because most edibles are plant-based, the body gathers water quickly resulting in regular use of the washroom.

While it may be discomforting, it is a good way of washing toxins out of the body quickly and more effectively. It leaves the body feeling fresh.

Constipation

At the beginning of the diet, the body may dehydrate due to frequent urination. Also, the increased amount of nuts may harden the contents of the colon resulting in constipation.

In this case, make sure to drink a lot of water, eat a lot of non-starchy vegetables, and take in enough salt to soften the colon's content.

Diabetic Ketoacidosis

For people with diabetes, when the body produces excessive ketones, an adequate production of insulin is short.

The body is then unable to transport the necessary amounts of glucose and sugars to the muscles and tissue, resulting in fatigue, shortness of breath, frequent urination, nausea, and vomiting, etc.

If diabetic, consult a doctor or dietician to help draw out appropriate keto meal plans to keep you healthy.

Keto Flu

Within the first few days of the keto diet, you are likely to experience flu-like symptoms; headaches, fatigue, dullness, irritability – these are fine. They are just your body's reaction to a change in dieting.

After four days, you will have adjusted to the new diet and feel active and vibrant.

Low Physical Performance

Energy levels may be low at the start since the body is deprived of carbohydrates and sugars. At this point, try not to be involved in high-intensity activities.

In a few days, your energy level will be back up, and you will be more energetic than you were before the diet.

Ask Your Doctor

Finally, you want to speak with your doctor before starting the keto diet. For pregnant women, health-related reason or if unsure that the keto is right for you, please talk with your doctor.

This is a safe diet and should technically work well for everyone; however, a little extra caution doesn't hurt.

About the Recipes

IN THIS BOOK YOU WILL FIND SIMPLE AND EASY RECIPES FOR EVERY MEAL.

Over half the recipes take less than 30 minutes to prepare, and whenever possible, I tried to minimize the number of pots and pans needed because I love for cleanup to be easy, too.

Each recipe in the book calls for just five main ingredients and uses some of these five pantry ingredients also: pink Himalayan salt, freshly ground black pepper, grass-fed ghee, olive oil, and grass-fed butter.

You'll also find the nutritional information as well as the macro breakdowns at the bottom of each recipe to help you make those notes I spoke about earlier.

Now, ready? Let's get some body-loving started!

Chapter 2: Breakfast

Swiss Cheese Chorizo Waffles

Prep + Cook Time: 30 minutes | Serves: 6

Ingredients

- 6 eggs
- 6 tbsp coconut milk
- 1 tsp Spanish spice mix
- Sea salt and black pepper, to taste
- 3 chorizo sausages, cooked, chopped
- 1 cup Gruyere cheese, shredded

Directions

1. Using a mixing bowl, beat the eggs, Spanish spice mix, black pepper, salt, and coconut milk.

2. Add in shredded cheese and chopped sausage. Use a nonstick cooking spray to spray a waffle iron.

3. Cook the egg mixture for 5 minutes.

4. Serve alongside homemade sugar-free tomato ketchup.

Per serving: Calories 316; Fat: 25g, Net Carbs: 1.5g, Protein: 20.2g

Breakfast Egg Muffins with Bacon

Prep + Cook Time: 30 minutes | Serves: 6

Ingredients

- 12 eggs
- ¼ cup coconut milk
- Salt and black pepper to taste
- 1 cup Colby cheese, grated
- 12 slices bacon
- 4 jalapeño peppers, seeded and minced

Directions

1. Preheat oven to 370°F.

2. Crack the eggs into a bowl and whisk with coconut milk until combined, season with salt and pepper, and evenly stir in the colby cheese.

3. Line each hole of a muffin tin with a slice of bacon and fill each with the egg mixture two-thirds way up.

4. Top with the jalapeño peppers and bake in the oven for 18 to 20 minutes or until puffed and golden. Remove, allow cooling for a few minutes, and serve with salad.

Per serving: Calories 302, Fat 23.7g, Net Carbs 3.2g, Protein 20g

Chorizo, Collard Greens and Avocado Eggs

Prep + Cook Time: 20 minutes | Serves: 4

Ingredients

- 1 tsp ghee
- 1 yellow onion, sliced
- 4 oz chorizo, sliced into thin rounds
- 1 cup chopped collard greens
- 1 ripe avocado, pitted, peeled, chopped
- 4 eggs
- Salt and black pepper to season

Directions

1. Preheat oven to 370°F. Melt ghee in a cast iron pan over medium heat and sauté the onion for 2 minutes. Add the chorizo and cook for 2 minutes more, flipping once.

2. Introduce the collard greens in batches with a splash of water to wilt, season lightly with salt, stir and cook for 3 minutes. Mix in the avocado and turn the heat off.

3. Create four holes in the mixture, crack the eggs into each hole, sprinkle with salt and black pepper, and slide the pan into the preheated oven and bake for 6 minutes until the egg whites are set or firm but with the yolks still runny.

4. Adjust the taste with salt and black pepper, and serve right away with low carb toasts.

Per serving: Calories 274, Fat 23g, Net Carbs 4g, Protein 13g

Coconut Almond Muffins

Prep + Cook Time: 30 minutes | Serves: 4

Ingredients

- 2 cups almond flour
- 2 tsp baking powder
- ½ tsp salt
- 8 oz ricotta cheese, softened
- ¼ cup melted butter
- 1 egg
- 1 cup unsweetened coconut milk

Directions

1. Preheat oven to 400°F and grease a 12-cup muffin tray with cooking spray. Mix the flour, baking powder, and salt in a large bowl.

2. In a separate bowl, beat the cream cheese and butter using a hand mixer and whisk in the egg and coconut milk. Fold in the flour, and spoon the batter into the muffin cups two-thirds way up.

3. Bake for 20 minutes until puffy at the top and golden brown, remove to a wire rack to cool slightly for 5 minutes before serving.

Per serving: Calories 320, Fat 30.6g, Net Carbs 6g, Protein 4g

Keto Breakfast Beef Stacks with Lemon

Prep + Cook Time: 16 minutes | Serves: 6

Ingredients

- 6 ground beef patties
- 4 tbsp olive oil
- 2 ripe avocados, pitted
- 2 tsp fresh lemon juice
- Salt and black pepper to taste
- 6 fresh eggs
- Red pepper flakes to garnish

Directions

1. In a skillet, warm the oil over medium heat and fry the patties about 8 minutes until lightly browned and firm. Put the patties in a plate.

2. Spoon the avocado into a bowl, mash with the lemon juice, and season with salt and black pepper. Spread the mash on the patties. Boil 3 cups of water in a wide pan over high heat, and reduce to simmer (don't boil).

3. Crack each egg into a small bowl and gently put the egg into the simmering water; poach for 2 to 3 minutes. Use a perforated spoon to remove from the water on a paper towel to dry. Repeat with the other 5 eggs. Top each stack with a poached egg, sprinkle with chili flakes, salt, pepper, and chives.

Per serving: Calories 378, Fat 23g, Net Carbs 5g, Protein 16g

Zucchini Quiche with Pancetta Breakfast

Prep + Cook Time: 25 minutes | Serves: 3

Ingredients

- 3 medium zucchinis, diced
- 6 pancetta slices
- 3 egg
- 3 tbsp olive oil
- 1 yellow onion, chopped
- 1 tbsp cilantro, chopped
- Salt to taste

Directions

1. Place the pancetta in a skillet and cook over medium heat for a few minutes, until the pancetta is crispy. Remove from the skillet and set aside.

2. Warm the olive oil and cook the onion until soft, for about 3-4 minutes, occasionally stirring. Add the zucchini, and cook for 10 more minutes until zucchini is brown and tender, but not mushy. Transfer to a plate and season with salt.

3. Crack the egg into the same skillet and fry over medium heat. Top the zucchini mixture with the pancetta slices and a fried egg. Serve hot, sprinkled with cilantro.

Per serving: Calories 423, Fat: 35.5g, Net Carbs: 6.6g, Protein: 17.4g

Bok Choy Squash Omelet with Sausage

Prep + Cook Time: 10 minutes | Serves: 1

Ingredients

- 2 eggs
- 1 cup bok choy, chopped
- 4 oz sausage, chopped
- 2 tbsp cotija cheese
- 4 ounces roasted squash
- 1 tbsp olive oil
- Salt and black pepper to taste

Directions

1. Beat the eggs in a bowl, season with salt and pepper and stir in the bok choy and the cotija cheese.

2. In another bowl, mash the squash. Add the squash to the egg mixture. Heat ¼ tbsp of olive oil in a pan over medium heat. Add sausage and cook until browned on all sides, turning occasionally.

3. Drizzle the remaining olive oil. Pour the egg mixture over. Cook for about 2 minutes per side until the eggs are thoroughly cooked and lightly browned. Remove the pan and run a spatula around the edges of the omelet; slide it onto a warm platter. Fold in half, and serve hot.

Per serving: Calories 558, Fat 51.7g, Net Carbs 7.5g, Protein 32.3g

Cauliflower and Ham Baked Eggs

Prep + Cook Time: 25 minutes | Serves: 4

Ingredients

- 2 heads cauliflower, cut into a small florets
- 2 green bell peppers, seeded and chopped
- ¼ cup chopped ham
- 2 tsp ghee
- 1 tsp dried oregano + extra to garnish
- Salt and black pepper to taste
- 8 fresh eggs

Directions

1. Preheat oven to 425°F.
2. Melt the ghee in a frying pan over medium heat; brown the ham, stirring frequently, about 3 minutes.
3. Arrange the cauliflower, bell peppers, and ham on a foil-lined baking sheet in a single layer, toss to combine; season with salt, oregano, and pepper.
4. Bake for 10 minutes until the vegetables have softened.
5. Remove, create eight indentations with a spoon, and crack an egg into each. Return to the oven and continue to bake for an additional 5 to 7 minutes until the egg whites are firm. Season with salt, pepper, and extra oregano, share the bake into four plates and serve with strawberry lemonade.

Per serving: Calories 344, Fat 28g, Net Carbs 4.2g, Protein 11g

Sausage and Grana Padano Egg Muffins

Prep + Cook Time: 10 minutes | Serves: 3

Ingredients

- 1 tsp butter, melted
- 6 eggs, separated into yolks and whites
- Salt and black pepper, to taste
- ½ tsp dried rosemary
- 1 cup Grana Padano cheese, grated
- 3 beef sausages, chopped

Directions

1. Set oven to 420°F. Lightly grease a muffin pan with the melted butter.
2. Use an electric mixer to beat the egg whites until there is a formation of stiff peaks. Add in sausages, cheese, and seasonings.
3. Add into muffin cups and bake for 4 minutes.
4. Place in an egg to each of the cups. Bake for an additional of 4 minutes. Allow cooling before serving.

Per serving: Calories 423; Fat: 34.1g, Net Carbs: 2.2g, Protein: 26.5g

Tofu Scramble with Mushrooms and Spinach

Prep + Cook Time: 30 minutes | Serves: 4

Ingredients

- 1 tbsp butter
- 1 cup sliced white mushrooms
- 2 cloves garlic, minced
- 16 oz firm tofu, pressed and crumbled
- Salt and black pepper to taste
- ½ cup spinach, sliced
- 6 fresh eggs

Directions

1. Melt the butter in a non-stick skillet over medium heat, and sauté the mushrooms for 5 minutes until they lose their liquid. Add the garlic and cook for 1 minute.

2. Crumble the tofu into the skillet, season with salt and pepper. Cook with continuous stirring for 6 minutes. Introduce the spinach in batches and cook to soften for about 7 minutes.

3. Crack the eggs into a bowl, whisk until well combined and creamy in color, and pour all over the kale. Use a spatula to immediately stir the eggs while cooking until scrambled and no more runny, about 5 minutes.

4. Adjust the taste with salt and pepper, plate, and serve with low carb crusted bread.

Per serving: Calories 469, Fat 39g, Net Carbs 5g, Protein 25g

Creamy Salmon Tortilla Wraps

Prep + Cook Time: 10 minutes + time refrigeration | Serves: 3

Ingredients

- 3 tbsp cottage cheese, softened
- 1 small lime, zested and juiced
- 3 tsp chopped fresh dill
- Salt and black pepper to taste
- 3 (7-inch) low carb tortillas
- 6 slices smoked salmon

Directions

1. In a bowl, mix the cottage cheese, lime juice, zest, dill, salt, and black pepper.

2. Lay each tortilla on a plastic wrap (just wide enough to cover the tortilla), spread with cottage cheese mixture, and top each (one) with two salmon slices. Roll up the tortillas and secure both ends by twisting.

3. Refrigerate for 2 hours, remove plastic, cut off both ends of each wrap, and cut wraps into half-inch wheels.

Per serving: Calories 250, Fat 16g, Net Carbs 7g, Protein 18g

Spinach and Fontina Cheese Nest Bites

Prep + Cook Time: 37 minutes | Serves: 4

Ingredients

- 1 tbsp olive oil
- 1 clove garlic, grated
- ½ lb spinach, chopped
- Salt and black pepper to taste
- 2 tbsp shredded fontina cheese
- 2 tbsp shredded pecorino romano cheese + some more
- 4 eggs

Directions

1. Preheat oven to 350°F. Warm the oil in a non-stick skillet over medium heat; add the garlic and sauté until softened for 2 minutes. Add the spinach to wilt about 5 minutes and season with salt and black pepper.

2. Top with pecorino romano and fontina cheeses, sauté for a further 2 minutes and turn the heat off. Allow complete cooling.

3. Grease a baking sheet with cooking spray, mold 4 (firm separate) spinach nests on the sheet, and crack an egg into each nest. Season with salt and black pepper, and sprinkle with Pecorino Romano cheese.

4. Bake for 15 minutes just until the egg whites have set and the yolks are still runny. Plate the nests and serve right away with toasts and coffee.

Per serving: Calories 230, Fat 17.5g, Net Carbs 4g, Protein 12g

Frittata with Spinach and Ricotta

Prep + Cook Time: 40 minutes | Serves: 4

Ingredients

- 5 ounces spinach
- 8 ounces crumbled ricotta cheese
- 1 pint halved cherry tomatoes
- 10 eggs
- 3 tbsp olive oil
- 4 green onions, diced
- Salt and black pepper, to taste

Directions

1. Preheat your oven to 350°F.

2. Drizzle the oil in a 2-quart casserole and place in the oven until heated. In a bowl, whisk the eggs along with the pepper and salt, until thoroughly combined.

3. Stir in the spinach, ricotta cheese, and green onions.

4. Pour the mixture into the casserole, top with the cherry tomatoes and place back in the oven. Bake for 25 minutes until your frittata is set in the middle.

5. When done, remove the casserole from the oven and run a spatula around the edges of the frittata; slide it onto a warm platter. Cut the frittata into wedges and serve with salad.

Per serving: Calories 461, Fat: 35g, Net Carbs: 6g, Protein: 26g

Chapter 3: Appetizers Snacks

Cream Cheese and Turkey Tortilla Rolls

Prep + Cook Time: 40 minutes | Serves: 4

Ingredients

- 8 oz softened cream cheese
- 10 oz turkey pastrami, sliced
- 10 canned pepperoncini peppers, sliced and drained

Directions

1. Lay a 12 x 12 plastic wrap on a flat surface and arrange the pastrami all over slightly overlapping each other. Spread the cheese on top of the salami layers and arrange the pepperoncini on top.

2. Hold two opposite ends of the plastic wrap and roll the pastrami. Twist both ends to tighten and refrigerate for 2 hours. Unwrap the salami roll and slice into 2-inch pinwheels. Serve.

Per serving: Calories 266, Fat 24g, Net Carbs 0g, Protein 13g

Savory Lime Fried Artichokes

Prep + Cook Time: 20 minutes | Serves: 4

Ingredients

- 12 fresh baby artichokes
- 2 tbsp lime juice
- 2 tbsp olive oil
- Salt to taste

Directions

1. Slice the artichokes vertically into narrow wedges. Drain on paper towels before frying.

2. Heat olive oil in a cast-iron skillet over high heat. Fry the artichokes until browned and crispy. Drain excess oil on paper towels. Sprinkle with salt and lime juice.

Per serving: Calories 35, Fat: 2.4g, Net Carbs: 2.9g, Protein: 2g

Baked Cheese Chicken

Prep + Cook Time: 30 minutes | Serves: 6

Ingredients

- 2 tbsp olive oil
- 8 oz cottage cheese, grated
- 1 lb ground chicken
- 1 cup buffalo sauce
- 1 cup ranch dressing
- 3 cups Monterey Jack cheese, grated

Directions

1. Preheat oven to 350°F. Lightly grease a baking sheet with a cooking spray.

2. Warm the oil in a skillet over medium heat and brown the chicken for a couple of minutes, take off the heat, and set aside.

3. Spread cottage cheese at the bottom of the baking sheet, top with chicken, pour buffalo sauce over, add ranch dressing, and sprinkle with Monterey Jack cheese.

4. Bake for 23 minutes until cheese has melted and golden brown on top. Remove and serve with veggie sticks or low carb crackers.

Per serving: Calories 216, Fat 16g, Net Carbs 3g, Protein 14g

Rosemary Cheese Chips with Guacamole

Prep + Cook Time: 10 minutes | Serves: 4

Ingredients

- 1 tbsp rosemary
- 1 cup Grana padano cheese, grated
- ¼ tsp sweet paprika
- ¼ tsp garlic powder
- 2 soft avocados, pitted and scooped
- 1 tomato, chopped
- Salt to taste

Directions

1. To make the chips, preheat oven to 350°F and line a baking sheet with parchment paper.

2. Mix Grana padano cheese, paprika, rosemary, and garlic powder evenly. Spoon 6 to 8 teaspoons on the baking sheet creating spaces between each mound. Flatten mounds with your hands. Bake for 5 minutes, cool, and remove with a spatula onto a plate.

3. To make the guacamole, mash avocado, with a fork in a bowl, add in tomato and continue to mash until mostly smooth. Season with salt.

4. Serve crackers with guacamole.

Per serving: Calories 229, Fat 20g, Net Carbs 2g, Protein 10g

Parmesan Green Bean Crisps

Prep + Cook Time: 30 minutes | Serves: 6

Ingredients

- ¼ cup Parmesan cheese, shredded
- ¼ cup pork rind crumbs
- 1 tsp minced garlic
- Salt and black pepper to taste
- 2 eggs
- 1 lb green beans, thread removed

Directions

1. Preheat oven to 425°F and line two baking sheets with foil. Grease with cooking spray and set aside.

2. Mix the Parmesan cheese, pork rinds, garlic, salt, and black pepper in a bowl. Beat the eggs in another bowl. Coat green beans in eggs, then cheese mixture and arrange evenly on the baking sheets.

3. Grease lightly with cooking spray and bake for 15 minutes to be crispy. Transfer to a wire rack to cool before serving. Serve with sugar-free tomato dip.

Per serving: Calories 210, Fat 19g, Net Carbs 3g, Protein 5g

Chili Baked Zucchini Sticks

Prep + Cook Time: 20 minutes | Serves: 4

Ingredients

- ¼ cup pork rind crumbs
- 1 tsp sweet paprika
- ¼ cup Pecorino Romano cheese, shredded
- Salt and chili pepper to taste
- 3 fresh eggs
- 2 zucchinis, cut into strips

Directions

1. Preheat oven to 425°F and line a baking sheet with foil. Grease with cooking spray and set aside. Mix the pork rinds, paprika, pecorino romano cheese, salt, and chili pepper in a bowl.

2. Beat the eggs in another bowl. Coat zucchini strips in egg, then in pecorino romano mixture, and arrange on the baking sheet. Grease lightly with cooking spray and bake for 15 minutes to be crispy.

3. To make the aioli, combine in a bowl mayonnaise, lemon juice, and garlic, and gently stir until everything is well incorporated. Add the lemon zest, adjust the seasoning and stir again. Cover and place in the refrigerator until ready to serve.

4. Arrange the zucchini strips on a serving plate and serve with garlic aioli for dipping.

Per serving: Calories 180, Fat 14g, Net Carbs 2g, Protein 6g

Cucumber-Turkey Canapes

Prep + Cook Time: 5 minutes | Serves: 6

Ingredients

- 2 cucumbers, sliced with a 3-inch thickness
- 2 cups small dices leftover turkey
- ¼ jalapeño pepper, seeded and minced
- 1 tbsp Dijon mustard
- ¼ cup mayonnaise
- Salt and black pepper to taste

Directions

1. Cut mid-level holes in cucumber slices with a knife and set aside.

2. Combine turkey, jalapeno, mustard, mayonnaise, salt, and black pepper to be evenly mixed. Fill cucumber holes with chicken mixture and serve.

Per serving: Calories 170, Fat 14g, Net Carbs 0g, Protein 10g

Paprika and Dill Deviled Eggs

Prep + Cook Time: 15 minutes | Serves: 4

Ingredients

- 1 tsp dill, chopped
- 8 large eggs
- 3 cups water
- Ice water bath
- 3 tbsp sriracha sauce
- 4 tbsp mayonnaise
- Salt to taste
- ¼ tsp sweet paprika

Directions

1. Bring eggs to boil in salted water in a pot over high heat, and then reduce the heat to simmer for 10 minutes.

2. Transfer eggs to an ice water bath, let cool completely and peel the shells.

3. Slice the eggs in half height wise and empty the yolks into a bowl.

4. Smash with a fork and mix in sriracha sauce, mayonnaise, and half of the paprika until smooth.

5. Spoon filling into a piping bag with a round nozzle and fill the egg whites to be slightly above the brim.

6. Garnish with remaining paprika and dill and serve immediately.

Per serving: Calories 195, Fat 19g, Net Carbs 1g, Protein 4g

Cheese and Garlic Crackers

Prep + Cook Time: 25 minutes | Serves: 6

Ingredients

- 1 ¼ cups coconut flour
- 1 ¼ cups Pecorino Romano cheese, grated
- Salt and black pepper to taste
- 1 tsp garlic powder
- ¼ cup ghee
- ¼ tsp sweet paprika
- ½ cup heavy cream
- Water as needed

Directions

1. Preheat the oven to 350°F.

2. Mix the coconut flour, pecorino romano cheese, salt, pepper, garlic powder, and paprika in a bowl. Add in the ghee and mix well. Top with the heavy cream and mix again until a smooth, thick mixture has formed. Add 1 to 2 tablespoon of water at this point, if it is too thick.

3. Place the dough on a cutting board and cover with plastic wrap. Use a rolling pin to spread out the dough into a light rectangle. Cut cracker squares out of the dough and arrange them on a baking sheet without overlapping. Bake for 20 minutes and transfer to a serving bowl after.

Per serving: Calories 115, Fat 3g, Net Carbs 0.7g, Protein 5g

Cheesy Chicken Wraps

Prep + Cook Time: 20 minutes | Serves: 8

Ingredients

- ¼ tsp garlic powder
- 8 ounces fontina cheese
- 8 raw chicken tenders
- ½ tsp black pepper
- 8 prosciutto slices

Directions

1. Pound the chicken until half an inch thick. Season with salt, pepper, and garlic powder. Cut the fontina cheese into 8 strips.

2. Place a slice of prosciutto on a flat surface. Place one chicken tender on top. Top with a fontina strip.

3. Roll the chicken and secure with previously soaked skewers.

4. Grill the wraps for 3 minutes per side.

Per serving: Calories 174, Fat: 10g, Net Carbs: 0.7g, Protein: 17g

Simple Stuffed Eggs with Mayonnaise

Prep + Cook Time: 30 minutes | Serves: 6

Ingredients

- 6 eggs
- 1 tbsp green tabasco
- ¼ cup mayonnaise
- Salt to taste
- 2 tbsp black olives, sliced

Directions

1. Place the eggs in a saucepan and cover with salted water.

2. Bring to a boil over medium heat. Boil for 10 minutes.

3. Place the eggs in an ice bath and let cool for 10 minutes.

4. Peel and slice in half lengthwise. Scoop out the yolks to a bowl; mash with a fork.

5. Whisk together the tabasco, mayonnaise, mashed yolks, and salt, in a bowl. Spoon this mixture into egg white.

6. Garnish with olive slices and serve.

Per serving: Calories 178, Fat: 17g, Net Carbs: 5g, Protein: 6g

Baked Chorizo with Cottage Cheese

Prep + Cook Time: 30 minutes | Serves: 6

Ingredients

- 7 ounces Spanish chorizo
- 4 ounces cottage cheese, pureed
- ¼ cup chopped parsley

Directions

1. Preheat your oven to 325 °F. Slice the chorizo into 30 slices

2. Line a baking dish with waxed paper. Bake the chorizo for 15 minutes until crispy. Remove from the oven and let cool. Arrange on a serving platter.

3. Top each slice with some cottage cheese.

4. Serve sprinkled with chopped parsley.

Per serving: Calories 172, Fat: 13g, Net Carbs: 0g, Protein: 5g

Chapter 4: Lunch

American Cobb Egg Salad in Lettuce Wraps

Prep + Cook Time: 25 minutes | Serves: 4

Ingredients

- 2 chicken breasts, cut into pieces
- 1 tbsp olive oil
- Salt and black pepper to season
- 6 large eggs
- 1 ½ cups water
- 2 tomatoes, seeded, chopped
- 6 tbsp cream cheese
- 1 head green lettuce, firm leaves removed for cups

Directions

1. Preheat oven to 400°F. Put the chicken pieces in a bowl, drizzle with olive oil, and sprinkle with salt and black pepper. Mix the ingredients until the chicken is well coated with the seasoning.

2. Put the chicken on a prepared baking sheet and spread out evenly. Slide the baking sheet in the oven and bake the chicken until cooked through and golden brown for 8 minutes, turning once.

3. Bring the eggs to boil in salted water in a pot over medium heat for 6 minutes. Run the eggs in cold water, peel, and chop into small pieces. Transfer to a salad bowl.

4. Remove the chicken from the oven when ready and add to the salad bowl. Include the tomatoes and cream cheese; mix evenly with a spoon.

5. Layer two lettuce leaves each as cups and fill with two tablespoons of egg salad each.

6. Serve with chilled blueberry juice.

Per serving: Calories 325, Fat 24.5g, Net Carbs 4g, Protein 21g

Thyme Tomato Soup

Prep + Cook Time: 20 minutes | Serves: 6

Ingredients

- 2 tbsp butter
- 2 large red onions, diced
- ½ cup raw cashew nuts, diced
- 2 (28-oz) cans tomatoes
- 1 tsp fresh thyme leaves + extra to garnish
- 1 ½ cups water
- Salt and black pepper to taste
- 1 cup half-and-half

Directions

1. Melt butter in a pot over medium heat and sauté the onion for 4 minutes until softened. Stir in the tomatoes, thyme, water, cashews, and season with salt and black pepper.

2. Cover and bring to simmer for 10 minutes until thoroughly cooked.

3. Open, turn the heat off, and puree the ingredients with an immersion blender. Adjust to taste and stir in the half-and-half. Spoon into soup bowls and serve.

Per serving: Calories 310, Fat 27g, Net Carbs 3g, Protein 11g

Pancetta Mashed Cauliflower

Prep + Cook Time: 40 minutes | Serves: 6

Ingredients

- 6 slices pancetta
- 3 heads cauliflower, leaves removed
- 2 cups water
- 2 tbsp melted butter
- ½ cup buttermilk
- Salt and black pepper to taste
- ¼ cup Colby cheese, grated
- 2 tbsp chopped chives

Directions

1. Preheat oven to 350°F. Fry pancetta in a heated skillet over medium heat for 5 minutes until crispy. Remove to a paper towel-lined plate, allow to cool, and crumble. Set aside and keep pancetta fat.

2. Boil cauli heads in water in a pot over high heat for 7 minutes, until tender. Drain and put in a bowl.

3. Include butter, buttermilk, salt, black pepper, and puree using a hand blender until smooth and creamy. Lightly grease a casserole dish with the pancetta fat and spread the mash in it.

4. Sprinkle with colby cheese and place under the broiler for 4 minutes on high until the cheese melts. Remove and top with pancetta and chopped chives. Serve with pan-seared scallops.

Per serving: Calories 312, Fat 25g, Net Carbs 6g, Protein 14g

Creamy Chicken Thighs

Prep + Cook Time: 50 minutes | Serves: 4

Ingredients

- 1 pound chicken thighs
- Salt and black pepper, to taste
- 1 tsp onion powder
- ¼ cup half-and-half
- 2 tbsp butter
- 2 tbsp sweet paprika

Directions

1. Using a bowl, combine the paprika with onion powder, pepper, and salt. Season chicken pieces with this mixture and lay on a lined baking sheet; bake for 40 minutes in the oven at 400°F. Split the chicken in serving plates, and set aside.

2. Add the cooking juices to a skillet over medium heat, and mix with the half-and-half and butter. Cook for 5-6 minutes until the sauce is thickened. Sprinkle the sauce over the chicken and serve.

Per serving: Calories 381, Fat 33g, Net Carbs 2.6g, Protein 31.3g

Eggplant Chicken Gratin With Swiss Cheese

Prep + Cook Time: 55 minutes | Serves: 4

Ingredients

- 3 tbsp butter
- 1 eggplant, chopped
- 2 tbsp Swiss cheese, grated
- Salt and black pepper, to taste
- 2 garlic cloves, minced
- 6 chicken thighs

Directions

1. Set a pan over medium heat and warm 1 tablespoon butter, place in the chicken thighs, season with pepper and salt, cook each side for 3 minutes and lay them in a baking dish.

2. In the same pan melt the rest of the butter and cook the garlic for 1 minute.

3. Stir in the eggplant, pepper, and salt, and cook for 10 minutes. Ladle this mixture over the chicken, spread with the cheese, set in the oven at 350°F, and bake for 30 minutes.

4. Turn on the oven's broiler, and broil everything for 2 minutes. Split among serving plates and enjoy.

Per serving: Calories 412, Fat 37g, Net Carbs 5g, Protein 34g

Pancetta Wrapped Chicken Rolls

Prep + Cook Time: 45 minutes | Serves: 4

Ingredients

- 1 tbsp fresh chives, chopped
- 8 ounces blue cheese
- 2 pounds chicken breasts, skinless, boneless, halved
- 12 pancetta slices
- 2 tomatoes, chopped
- Salt and ground black pepper, to taste

Directions

1. Set a pan over medium heat, place in the pancetta, cook until halfway done, remove to paper towels, and drain the grease. Using a bowl, stir together the blue cheese, chives, tomatoes, pepper, and salt.

2. Use a meat tenderizer to flatten the chicken breasts well, season and lay the cream cheese mixture on top. Roll them up, and wrap each in a pancetta slice. Place the wrapped chicken breasts in a greased baking dish, and roast in the oven at 370°F for 30 minutes. Serve on top of wilted kale.

Per serving: Calories 623, Fat 48g, Net Carbs 5g, Protein 38g

Grilled BBQ Pork Chops

Prep + Cook Time: 1 hour 47 minutes | Serves: 4

Ingredients

- 4 (6 oz) thick-cut pork loin chops, boneless
- ½ cup sugar-free BBQ sauce
- 1 tsp black pepper
- 1 tbsp erythritol
- ½ tsp ginger powder
- ½ tsp garlic powder
- 2 tsp smoked paprika

Directions

1. In a bowl, mix the black pepper, erythritol, ginger powder, ½ tsp garlic powder, and smoked paprika, and rub the pork chops on all sides with the mixture. Then, cover the pork chops with plastic wraps and place it in the refrigerator to marinate for 1 hour 30 minutes.

2. Preheat the grill to 450°F. Unwrap the meat, place on the grill grate, and cook for 2 minutes per side. Reduce the heat and brush the BBQ sauce on the meat, cover the lid, and grill them for 5 minutes.

3. Open the lid, turn the meat and brush again with barbecue sauce. Continue cooking covered for 5 minutes. Remove the meat to a serving platter and serve with steamed vegetables.

Per serving: Calories 363, Fat 26.6g, Net Carbs 0g, Protein 34.1g

Chicken Breasts with Jarred Pickle Juice

Prep + Cook Time: 20 minutes | Serves: 4

Ingredients

- 2 chicken breasts, cut into strips
- 4 ounces chicken crisps, crushed
- 2 cups coconut oil
- 16 ounces jarred pickle juice
- 2 eggs, whisked

Directions

1. Using a bowl, combine the chicken breast pieces with pickle juice and refrigerate for 12 hours while covered.

2. Set the eggs in a bowl, and chicken crisps in a separate one. Dip the chicken pieces in the eggs, and then in chicken crisps, and ensure they are well coated.

3. Set a pan over medium-high heat and warm oil, fry the chicken for 3 minutes on each side, remove to paper towels, drain the excess grease, and enjoy.

Per serving: Calories 387, Fat 16g, Net Carbs 2.5g, Protein 23g

Baked Tenderloin with Lime Chimichurri

Prep + Cook Time: 64 minutes | Serves: 4

Ingredients

Lime chimichurri

- 1 lime, juiced
- ¼ cup chopped mint leaves
- ¼ cup rosemary leaves, chopped
- 2 cloves garlic, minced
- ¼ cup olive oil
- Salt to taste

Pork

- 1 (4 lb) pork tenderloin
- Salt and black pepper to season
- Olive oil for rubbing

Directions

1. Make the lime chimichurri to have the flavors incorporate while the pork cooks.

2. In a bowl, mix the mint, rosemary, and garlic. Then, add the lime juice, olive oil, and salt, and combine well. Set the sauce aside in room temperature.

3. Preheat the charcoal grill to 450°F in medium-high heat creating a direct heat area and indirect heat area. Rub the pork with olive oil, season with salt and pepper. Place the meat over direct heat and sear for 3 minutes on each side, after which, move to the indirect heat area.

4. Close the lid and cook for 25 minutes on one side, then open, turn the meat, and grill closed for 20 minutes on the other side. Remove the pork from the grill and let it sit for 5 minutes before slicing. Spoon lemon chimichurri over the pork and serve with a fresh salad.

Per serving: Calories 388, Fat 18g, Net Carbs 2.1g, Protein 28g

Baked Pulled Pork Tenderloin with Avocado

Prep + Cook Time: 55 minutes | Serves: 12

Ingredients

- 4 pounds pork tenderloin
- 1 tbsp avocado oil
- ½ cup beef stock
- ¼ cup jerk seasoning
- 6 avocado, sliced

Directions

1. Rub the pork shoulder with jerk seasoning, and set in a greased baking dish.

2. Pour in the stock, and cook for 1 hour 45 minutes in your oven at 350°F covered with aluminium foil.

3. Discard the foil and cook for another 20 minutes. Leave to rest for 30 minutes, and shred it with 2 forks.

4. Serve topped with avocado slices.

Per serving: Calories 567, Fat 42.6g, Net Carbs 4.1g, Protein 42g

Roasted Stuffed Lamb Leg with Pine Nuts Rosemary

Prep + Cook Time: 1 hour 4 minutes | Serves: 4

Ingredients

- 1 lb rolled lamb leg, boneless
- 1 ½ cups rosemary, chopped
- 5 tbsp pine nuts, chopped
- ½ cup green olives, pitted and chopped
- 3 cloves garlic, minced
- Salt and black pepper to taste

Directions

1. Preheat the oven to 450°F. In a bowl, combine the rosemary, pine nuts, olives, and garlic. Season with salt and black pepper.

2. Untie the lamb flat onto a chopping board, spread the rosemary mixture all over, and rub the spice into the meat. Roll the lamb over the spice mixture and tie it together using 3 to 4 strings of butcher's twine.

3. Place the lamb onto a baking dish and cook in the oven for 10 minutes. Reduce the heat to 350°F and continue cooking for 40 minutes.

4. When ready, transfer the meat to a cleaned chopping board; let it rest for 10 minutes before slicing.

5. Serve with a side of equally roasted capsicums and root vegetables.

Per serving: Calories 547, Fat 37.7g, Net Carbs 2.2g, Protein 42.7g

Pork Medallions with Pancetta

Prep + Cook Time: 55 minutes | Serves: 4

Ingredients

- 2 onions, chopped
- 6 pancetta slices, chopped
- ½ cup vegetable stock
- Salt and black pepper, to taste
- 1 pound pork loin, cut into medallions

Directions

1. Set a pan over medium heat, stir in the pancetta, cook until crispy, and remove to a plate. Add onions, some pepper, and salt, and cook for 5 minutes; set to the same plate with pancetta.

2. Add the pork medallions to the pan, season with pepper and salt, brown for 3 minutes on each side, turn, reduce heat to medium, and cook for 7 minutes. Stir in the stock, and cook for 2 minutes. Return the pancetta and onions to the pan and cook for 1 minute.

Per serving: Calories 325, Fat 18g, Net Carbs 6g, Protein 36g

Herbed Veal Rack

Prep + Cook Time: 50 minutes | Serves: 4

Ingredients

- 12 ounces veal rack
- 2 fennel bulbs, sliced
- Salt and black pepper, to taste
- 3 tbsp olive oil
- ½ cup apple cider vinegar
- 1 tsp herbs de Provence
- 1 tbsp swerve

Directions

1. In a bowl, mix the fennel with 2 tbsp of oil, swerve, and vinegar, toss to coat well, and set to a baking dish. Season with herbs de Provence, pepper and salt, and cook in the oven at 400°F for 15 minutes.

2. Sprinkle pepper and salt to the veal, place into an oiled pan over medium-high heat, and cook for a couple of minutes.

3. Place the veal to the baking dish with the fennel, and bake for 20 minutes.

4. Split everything among plates and enjoy.

Per serving: Calories 230, Fat 11.3g, Net Carbs 5.2g, Protein 19g

Garlic and Parsley Shrimp

Prep + Cook Time: 22 minutes | Serves: 6

Ingredients

- ½ cup ghee, divided
- 2 lb shrimp, peeled and deveined
- Sea salt and black pepper to taste
- ¼ tsp sweet paprika
- 1 tbsp minced garlic
- 3 tbsp water
- 1 lemon, zested and juiced
- 2 tbsp chopped parsley

Directions

1. Melt half of the ghee in a large skillet over medium heat, season the shrimp with salt, pepper, paprika, and add to the ghee.

2. Stir in the garlic and cook the shrimp for 4 minutes on both sides until pink. Remove into a bowl and set aside.

3. Put the remaining ghee in the skillet; include the lemon zest, juice, and water. Cook until the ghee has melted about 1 minute.

4. Add the shrimp, parsley, and adjust taste with salt and black pepper. Cook for 2 minutes on low heat. Serve the shrimp and sauce with squash pasta.

Per serving: Calories 258, Fat 22g, Net Carbs 2g, Protein 13g

Creamy Salmon with Lemon

Prep + Cook Time: 25 minutes | Serves: 4

Ingredients

- 1 cup sour cream
- ½ tbsp minced dill
- ½ lemon, zested and juiced
- Salt and black pepper to season
- 4 salmon steaks
- ½ cup grated Pecorino Romano cheese

Directions

1. Preheat oven to 400°F and line a baking sheet with parchment paper; set aside. In a bowl, mix the sour cream, dill, lemon zest, Juice, salt, and pepper, and set aside.

2. Season the fish with salt and black pepper, drizzle lemon juice on both sides of the fish and arrange them in the baking sheet. Spread the sour cream mixture on each fish and sprinkle with Pecorino Romano cheese.

3. Bake fish for 15 minutes and after broil the top for 2 minutes with a close watch for a nice a brown color. Plate the fish and serve with buttery green beans.

Per serving: Calories 288, Fat 23.4g, Net Carbs 1.2g, Protein 16.2g

Fish Taco Bowl with Broccoli, Avocado and Cabbage

Prep + Cook Time: 17 minutes | Serves: 4

Ingredients

- 2 cups broccoli, chopped
- Water for sprinkling
- 2 tsp ghee
- 4 tilapia fillets, cut into cubes
- ¼ tsp taco seasoning
- Salt and chili pepper to taste
- ¼ head red cabbage, shredded
- 1 ripe avocado, pitted and chopped

Directions

1. Sprinkle broccoli in a bowl with a little water and microwave for 3 minutes. Fluff after with a fork and set aside.

2. Melt ghee in a skillet over medium heat, rub the tilapia with the taco seasoning, salt, and chili pepper, and fry until brown on all sides, for about 8 minutes in total.

3. Transfer to a plate and set aside. In 4 serving bowls, share the broccoli, cabbage, fish, and avocado. Serve with chipotle lime sour cream dressing.

Per serving: Calories 269, Fat 23.4g, Net Carbs 4g, Protein 16.5g

Broccoli Tips with Lemon Pork Chops

Prep + Cook Time: 27 minutes | Serves: 6

Ingredients

- 3 tbsp lemon juice
- 3 cloves garlic, pureed
- 1 tbsp olive oil
- 6 pork loin chops
- 1 tbsp butter
- 1 lb fresh broccoli tips, halved
- 2 tbsp white wine
- Salt and black pepper to taste

Directions

1. Preheat broiler to 400°F and mix the lemon juice, garlic, salt, pepper, and oil in a bowl.

2. Brush the pork with the mixture, place in a baking sheet, and cook for 6 minutes on each side until browned. Share into 6 plates and make the side dish.

3. Melt butter in a small wok or pan and cook in broccoli tips for 5 minutes until tender. Drizzle with white wine, sprinkle with salt and black pepper and cook for another 5 minutes.

4. Ladle broccoli tips to the side of the chops and serve with a hot sauce.

Per serving: Calories 549, Fat 48g, Net Carbs 2g, Protein 26g

Beef Stir-Fry with Peanut Sauce

Prep + Cook Time: 23 minutes | Serves: 4

Ingredients

- 1 ½ tbsp ghee
- 2 lb beef loin, cut into strips
- Pink salt and chili pepper to taste
- 2 tsp ginger-garlic paste
- ¼ cup chicken broth
- 5 tbsp peanut butter
- 2 cups mixed stir-fry vegetables

Directions

1. Melt the ghee in a wok and mix the beef with salt, chili pepper, and ginger-garlic paste. Pour the beef into the wok and cook for 6 minutes until no longer pink.

2. Mix the peanut butter with some broth to be smooth, add to the beef and stir; cook for 2 minutes.

3. Pour in the remaining broth, cook for 4 minutes, and add the mixed veggies. Simmer for 5 minutes.

4. Adjust the taste with salt and black pepper, and spoon the stir-fry to a side of cilantro cauli rice.

Per serving: Calories 571, Fat 49g, Net Carbs 1g, Protein 22.5g

Spicy Grilled Pork Spareribs

Prep + Cook Time: 32 minutes | Serves: 4

Ingredients

- 2 tbsp erythritol
- Salt and black pepper to taste
- 1 tbsp olive oil
- 3 tsp cayenne powder
- 1 tsp garlic powder
- 1 lb pork spareribs
- 4 tbsp sugar-free BBQ sauce + extra for serving

Directions

1. Mix the erythritol, salt, pepper, oil, cayenne, and garlic powder. Brush on the meaty sides of the ribs and wrap in foil. Sit for 30 minutes to marinate.

2. Preheat oven to 400°F, place wrapped ribs on a baking sheet, and cook for 40 minutes to be cooked through. Remove ribs and aluminium foil, brush with BBQ sauce, and brown under the broiler for 10 minutes on both sides.

3. Slice and serve with extra BBQ sauce and lettuce tomato salad.

Per serving: Calories 395, Fat 33g, Net Carbs 3g, Protein 21g

Beef Stuffed Zucchini Boats

Prep + Cook Time: 25 minutes | Serves: 4

Ingredients

- 4 zucchinis
- 2 tbsp olive oil
- 1 ½ lb ground beef
- 1 medium red onion, chopped
- 2 tbsp chopped pimiento
- Salt and black pepper to taste
- 1 cup Colby cheese, grated

Directions

1. Preheat oven to 350°F.

2. Lay the zucchinis on a flat surface, trim off the ends and cut in half lengthwise. Scoop out pulp from each half with a spoon to make shells. Chop the pulp.

3. Heat oil in a skillet; add the ground beef, red onion, pimiento, and zucchini pulp, and season with salt and black pepper. Cook for 6 minutes while stirring to break up lumps until beef is no longer pink. Turn the heat off. Spoon the beef into the boats and sprinkle with colby cheese.

4. Place on a greased baking sheet and cook to melt the cheese for 15 minutes until zucchini boats are tender. Take out, cool for 2 minutes, and serve warm.

Per serving: Calories 335, Fat 24g, Net Carbs 7g, Protein 18g

Feta Bacon Green Salad

Prep + Cook Time: 15 minutes | Serves: 4

Ingredients

- 2 (8 oz) pack mixed salad greens
- 8 strips bacon
- 1 ½ cups feta cheese, crumbled
- 1 tbsp white wine vinegar
- 3 tbsp extra virgin olive oil
- Salt and black pepper to taste

Directions

1. Pour the salad greens in a salad bowl; set aside. Fry bacon strips in a skillet over medium heat for 6 minutes, until browned and crispy. Chop the bacon and scatter over the salad. Add in half of the cheese, toss and set aside.

2. In a small bowl, whisk the white wine vinegar, olive oil, salt, and black pepper until dressing is well combined. Drizzle half of the dressing over the salad, toss, and top with remaining cheese. Divide salad into four plates and serve with crusted chicken fries along with remaining dressing.

Per serving: Calories 205, Fat 20g, Net Carbs 2g, Protein 4g

Haddock in Garlic Butter Sauce

Prep + Cook Time: 20 minutes | Serves: 6

Ingredients

- 2 tsp olive oil
- 6 haddock fillets
- Salt and black pepper to taste
- 4 tbsp salted butter
- 4 cloves garlic, minced
- ¼ cup lemon juice
- 3 tbsp white wine
- 2 tbsp chopped chives

Directions

1. Heat the oil in a skillet over medium heat and season the haddock with salt and black pepper. Fry the fillets in the oil for 4 minutes on one side, flip and cook for 1 minute. Take out, plate, and set aside.

2. In another skillet over low heat, melt the butter and sauté the garlic for 3 minutes. Add the lemon juice, wine, and chives. Season with salt, black pepper, and cook for 3 minutes until the wine slightly reduces. Put the fish in the skillet, spoon sauce over, cook for 30 seconds and turn the heat off.

3. Divide fish into 6 plates, top with sauce, and serve with buttered green beans.

Per serving: Calories 264, Fat 17.3g, Net Carbs 2.3g, Protein 20g

Broccoli and Fish Gratin

Prep + Cook Time: 40 minutes | Serves: 4

Ingredients

- 2 salmon fillets, cubed
- 3 white fish, cubed
- 1 broccoli, cut into florets
- 1 tbsp butter, melted
- Pink salt and black pepper to taste
- 1 cup crème fraiche
- ¼ cup grated pecorino romano cheese
- Grated Pecorino Romano cheese for topping

Directions

1. Preheat oven to 400°F and grease an 8 x 8-casserole dish with cooking spray. Toss the fish cubes and broccoli in butter and season with salt and black pepper to taste. Spread in the greased dish.

2. Mix the crème fraiche with pecorino romano cheese, pour and smear the cream on the fish, and sprinkle with some more pecorino romano cheese.

3. Bake for 25 to 30 minutes until golden brown on top, take the dish out, sit for 5 minutes and spoon into plates. Serve with lemon-mustard asparagus.

Per serving: Calories 354, Fat 17g, Net Carbs 4g, Protein 28g

Coconut Crab Cakes

Prep + Cook Time: 15 minutes | Serves: 8

Ingredients

- 2 tbsp coconut oil
- 1 tbsp lime juice
- 1 cup lump crab meat
- 2 tsp Dijon mustard
- 1 egg, beaten
- 1 ½ tbsp coconut flour
- 1 tbsp cilantro, chopped

Directions

1. In a bowl to the crabmeat add all the ingredients, except for coconut oil; mix well to combine. Make patties out of the mixture.

2. Melt the coconut oil in a skillet over medium heat. Add the crabmeat patties and cook for about 2-3 minutes per side.

Per serving: Calories 215, Fat: 11.5g, Net Carbs: 3.6g, Protein: 15.3g

Tofu and Spinach Zucchini Lasagna

Prep + Cook Time: 50 minutes | Serves: 4

Ingredients

*   2 zucchinis, sliced
*   Salt and black pepper to taste
*   2 cups cream cheese
*   2 cups tofu cheese, shredded
*   3 cups tomato sauce
*   1 cup packed baby spinach

Directions

1. Preheat oven to 370°F and grease a baking dish with cooking spray.

2. Put the zucchini slices in a colander and sprinkle with salt. Let sit and drain liquid for 5 minutes and pat dry with paper towels. Mix the cream cheese, tofu cheese, salt, and pepper to evenly combine and spread ¼ cup of the mixture in the bottom of the baking dish.

3. Layer a third of the zucchini slices on top spread 1 cup of tomato sauce over, and scatter one-third cup of spinach on top. Repeat the layering process two more times to exhaust the ingredients while making sure to layer with the last ¼ cup of cheese mixture finally.

4. Grease one end of foil with cooking spray and cover the baking dish with the foil. Bake for 35 minutes, remove foil, and bake further for 5 to 10 minutes or until the cheese has a nice golden brown color. Remove the dish, sit for 5 minutes, make slices of the lasagna, and serve warm.

Per serving: Calories 390, Fat 39g, Net Carbs 2g, Protein 7g

Cheese Scallops with Chorizo

Prep + Cook Time: 15 minutes | Serves: 4

Ingredients

- 2 tbsp ghee
- 16 fresh scallops
- 8 ounces chorizo, chopped
- 1 red bell pepper, seeds removed, sliced
- 1 cup red onions, finely chopped
- 1 cup Parmesan cheese, grated
- Salt and black pepper to taste

Directions

1. Melt half of the ghee in a skillet over medium heat, and cook the onion and bell pepper for 5 minutes until tender. Add the chorizo and stir-fry for another 3 minutes. Remove and set aside.

2. Pat dry the scallops with paper towels, and season with salt and pepper. Add the remaining ghee to the skillet and sear the scallops for 2 minutes on each side to have a golden brown color.

3. Add the chorizo mixture back and warm through. Transfer to serving platter and top with Parmesan cheese.

Per serving: Calories 491, Fat 32g, Net Carbs 5g, Protein 36g

Seitan Kabobs with BBQ Sauce

Prep + Cook Time: 2 hours 26 minutes | Serves: 4

Ingredients

- 10 oz seitan, cut into chunks
- 1 ½ cups water
- 1 red onion, cut into chunks
- 1 red bell pepper, cut chunks
- 1 yellow bell pepper, cut into chunks
- 2 tbsp olive oil
- 1 cup sugar-free barbecue sauce

Directions

1. Bring the water to boil in a pot over medium heat and once it has boiled, turn the heat off, and add the seitan. Cover the pot and let the tempeh steam for 5 minutes to remove its bitterness.

2. Drain the seitan after. Pour the barbecue sauce in a bowl, add the seitan to it, and coat with the sauce. Cover the bowl and marinate in the fridge for 2 hours.

3. Preheat a grill to 350°F, and thread the seitan, yellow bell pepper, red bell pepper, and onion.

4. Brush the grate of the grill with olive oil, place the skewers on it, and brush with barbecue sauce. Cook the kabobs for 3 minutes on each side while rotating and brushing with more barbecue sauce. Once ready, transfer the kabobs to a plate and serve with lemon cauli couscous and a tomato sauce.

Per serving: Calories 228, Fat 15g, Net Carbs 3.6g, Protein 13.2g

Spinach and Strawberry Salad with Blue Cheese

Prep + Cook Time: 20 minutes | Serves: 2

Ingredients

- 4 cups spinach
- 4 strawberries, sliced
- ½ cup flaked almonds
- 1 ½ cups gorgonzola cheese, grated
- 4 tbsp raspberry vinaigrette
- Salt and black pepper, to taste

Directions

1. Preheat your oven to 400°F. Arrange the grated gorgonzola cheese in two circles on two pieces of parchment paper. Place in the oven and bake for 10 minutes.

2. Find two same bowls, place them upside down, and carefully put the parchment paper on top to give the cheese a bowl-like shape. Let cool that way for 15 minutes. Divide spinach among the bowls and drizzle with vinaigrette.

3. Top with almonds and strawberries.

Per serving: Calories 445, Fat: 34.2g, Net Carbs: 5.3g, Protein: 33g

Spicy Smoked Mackerel Cakes

Prep + Cook Time: 30 minutes | Serves: 6

Ingredients

- 1 rutabaga, peeled and diced
- 1 ½ cups water
- Salt and chili pepper to taste
- 3 tbsp olive oil + for rubbing
- 4 smoked mackerel steaks, bones removed, flaked
- 3 eggs, beaten
- 2 tbsp mayonnaise
- 1 tbsp pork rinds, crushed

Directions

1. Bring the rutabaga to boil in salted water in a saucepan over medium heat for 8 minutes or until tender. Drain the rutabaga through a colander, transfer to a mixing bowl, and mash the lumps.

2. Add the mackerel, eggs, mayonnaise, pork rinds, salt, and chili pepper. With gloves on your hands, mix and make 6 compact patties.

3. Heat olive oil in a skillet over medium heat and fry the patties for 3 minutes on each side to be golden brown. Remove onto a wire rack to cool. Serve cakes with sesame lime dipping sauce.

Per serving: Calories 324, Fat 27.1g, Net Carbs 2.2g, Protein 16g

Prawns, Avocado and Cauliflower Salad

Prep + Cook Time: 30 minutes | Serves: 6

Ingredients

- 1 cauliflower head, florets only
- 1 lb medium-sized prawns
- ¼ cup + 1 tbsp olive oil
- 1 avocado, chopped
- 3 tbsp chopped dill
- ¼ cup lemon juice
- 2 tbsp lemon zest

Directions

1. Heat 1 tbsp olive oil in a skillet and cook the prawns until opaque, about 8-10 minutes.

2. Place the cauliflower florets in a microwave-safe bowl, and microwave for 5 minutes. Place the prawns, cauliflower, and avocado in a large bowl.

3. Whisk together the remaining olive oil, lemon zest, juice, dill, and some salt and pepper, in another bowl. Pour the dressing over, toss to combine and serve immediately.

Per serving: Calories 214, Fat: 17g, Net Carbs: 5g, Protein: 15g

Cauliflower Soup with Chorizo Sausage

Prep + Cook Time: 40 minutes | Serves: 4

Ingredients

- 1 cauliflower head, chopped
- 1 rutabaga, chopped
- 3 tbsp ghee
- 1 chorizo sausage, sliced
- 2 cups chicken broth
- 1 small onion, chopped
- 2 cups water
- Salt and black pepper, to taste

Directions

1. Melt 2 tbsp. of the ghee in a large pot over medium heat. Stir in onion and cook until soft and golden, about 3-4 minutes. Add cauliflower and rutabaga, and cook for another 5 minutes.

2. Pour the broth and water over. Bring to a boil, simmer covered, and cook for about 20 minutes until the vegetables are tender. Remove from heat.

3. Melt the remaining butter in a skillet. Add the chorizo sausage and cook for 5 minutes until crispy. Puree the soup with a hand blender until smooth. Taste and adjust the seasonings.

4. Serve the soup in deep bowls topped with the chorizo sausage.

Per serving: Calories 251, Fat: 19.1g, Net Carbs: 5.7g, Protein: 10g

Vegetable Stew

Prep + Cook Time: 32 minutes | Serves: 4

Ingredients

- 2 tbsp ghee
- 1 tbsp onion garlic puree
- 4 medium carrots, peeled and chopped
- 1 large head broccoli, cut into florets
- 2 cups green beans, halved
- Salt and black pepper to taste
- 1 cup water
- 1 ½ cups heavy cream

Directions

1. Melt ghee in a saucepan over medium heat and sauté onion-garlic puree to be fragrant, 2 minutes.

2. Stir in carrots, broccoli, and green beans, salt, and pepper, add the water, stir again, and cook the vegetables on low heat for 25 minutes to soften. Mix in the heavy cream to be incorporated, turn the heat off, and adjust the taste with salt and pepper. Serve the stew with almond flour bread.

Per serving: Calories 310, Fat 26.4g, Net Carbs 6g, Protein 8g

Grana Padano Roasted Cabbage

Prep + Cook Time: 25 minutes | Serves: 4

Ingredients

- Cooking spray
- 1 large head green cabbage
- 4 tbsp melted butter
- 1 tsp garlic powder
- Salt and black pepper to taste
- 1 cup grated Grana Padano cheese
- Grated Parmesan cheese for topping
- Grated Grana Padano cheese for topping
- 1 tbsp chopped parsley to garnish

Directions

1. Preheat oven to 400°F, line a baking sheet with foil, and grease with cooking spray.

2. Stand the cabbage and run a knife from the top to bottom to cut the cabbage into wedges. Remove stems and wilted leaves. Mix the butter, garlic, salt, and black pepper until evenly combined.

3. Brush the mixture on all sides of the cabbage wedges and sprinkle with Grana Padano cheese.

4. Place on the baking sheet, and bake for 20 minutes to soften the cabbage and melt the cheese. Remove the cabbages when golden brown, plate and sprinkle with extra cheese and parsley. Serve warm with pan-glazed tofu.

Per serving: Calories 268, Fat 19.3g, Net Carbs 4g, Protein 17.5g

Asparagus and Shrimp Curry Soup

Prep + Cook Time: 20 minutes | Serves: 4

Ingredients

- 2 tbsp ghee
- 1 lb jumbo shrimp, peeled and deveined
- 2 tsp ginger-garlic puree
- 2 tbsp red curry paste
- 6 oz coconut milk
- Salt and chili pepper to taste
- 1 bunch asparagus

Directions

1. Melt ghee in a medium saucepan over medium heat. Add the shrimp, season with salt and pepper, and cook until they are opaque, 2 to 3 minutes. Remove shrimp to a plate. Add the ginger-garlic puree and red curry paste to the ghee and sauté for 2 minutes until fragrant.

2. Stir in the coconut milk; add the shrimp, salt, chili pepper, and asparagus . Cook for 4 minutes. Reduce the heat to a simmer and cook an additional 3 minutes, occasionally stirring. Adjust taste, fetch soup into serving bowls, and serve with cauli rice.

Per serving: Calories 375, Fat 35.4g, Net Carbs 2g, Protein 9g

Colby Cauliflower Soup with Pancetta Chips

Prep + Cook Time: 25 minutes | Serves: 4

Ingredients

- 2 tbsp ghee
- 1 onion, chopped
- 2 head cauliflower, cut into florets
- 2 cups water
- Salt and black pepper to taste
- 3 cups almond milk
- 1 cup Colby cheese, shredded
- 3 pancetta strips

Directions

1. Melt the ghee in a saucepan over medium heat and sauté the onion for 3 minutes until fragrant. Include the cauli florets, sauté for 3 minutes to slightly soften, add the water, and season with salt and black pepper. Bring to a boil, and then reduce the heat to low. Cover and cook for 10 minutes.

2. Puree cauliflower with an immersion blender until the ingredients are evenly combined and stir in the almond milk and cheese until the cheese melts. Adjust taste with salt and black pepper. In a non-stick skillet over high heat, fry the pancetta, until crispy. Divide soup between serving bowls, top with crispy pancetta, and serve hot.

Per serving: Calories 402, Fat 37g, Net Carbs 6g, Protein 8g

Caesar Salad with Poached Eggs Smoked Salmon

Prep + Cook Time: 15 minutes | Serves: 4

Ingredients

- 3 cups water
- 8 eggs
- 2 cups torn romaine lettuce
- ½ cup chopped smoked salmon
- 6 slices pancetta
- 2 tbsp heinz low carb caesar dressing

Directions

1. Boil the water in a pot over medium heat for 5 minutes and bring to simmer. Crack each egg into a small bowl and gently slide into the water. Poach for 2 to 3 minutes, remove with a perforated spoon, transfer to a paper towel to dry, and plate.

2. Poach the remaining 7 eggs. Put the pancetta in a skillet and fry over medium heat until browned and crispy, about 6 minutes, turning once. Remove, allow cooling, and chop in small pieces.

3. Toss the lettuce, smoked salmon, pancetta, and caesar dressing in a salad bowl. Divide the salad into 4 plates, top with two eggs each, and serve immediately.

Per serving: Calories 260, Fat 21g, Net Carbs 5g, Protein 8g

Cheese Brussels Sprouts Salad

Prep + Cook Time: 35 minutes | Serves: 6

Ingredients

- 2 lb Brussels sprouts, halved
- 3 tbsp olive oil
- Salt and black pepper to taste
- 2 ½ tbsp balsamic vinegar
- ¼ red cabbage, shredded
- 1 tbsp Dijon mustard
- 1 cup Parmesan cheese, grated
- 2 tbsp pumpkin seeds, toasted

Directions

1. Preheat oven to 400°F and line a baking sheet with foil. Toss the brussels sprouts with olive oil, a little salt, black pepper, and balsamic vinegar, in a bowl, and spread on the baking sheet in an even layer.

2. Bake until tender on the inside and crispy on the outside, about 20 to 25 minutes.

3. Transfer to a salad bowl and add the red cabbage, Dijon mustard and half of the cheese. Mix until well combined. Sprinkle with the remaining cheese and pumpkin seeds, share the salad onto serving plates, and serve with syrup-grilled salmon.

Per serving: Calories 210, Fat 18g, Net Carbs 6g, Protein 4g

Swiss Pork Patties with Salad

Prep + Cook Time: 25 minutes | Serves: 4

Ingredients

- 1 lb ground pork
- Salt and black pepper to season
- 1 tbsp olive oil
- 2 hearts romaine lettuce, torn into pieces
- 2 firm tomatoes, sliced
- ¼ red onion, sliced
- 3 oz Swiss cheese, shredded

Directions

1. Season the pork with salt and black pepper, mix and make medium-sized patties out of them.
2. Heat the oil in a skillet over medium heat and fry the patties on both sides for 10 minutes until browned and cook within.
3. Transfer to a wire rack to drain oil. When cooled, cut into quarters.
4. Mix the lettuce, tomatoes, and onion in a salad bowl, season with a little oil, salt, and pepper. Toss and add the pork on top.
5. Melt the cheese in the microwave for about 90 seconds.
6. Drizzle the cheese over the salad and serve.

Per serving: Calories 310, Fat 23g, Net Carbs 2g, Protein 22g

Hazelnut Cod Fillets

Prep + Cook Time: 30 minutes | Serves: 2

Ingredients

- 2 cod fillets
- 2 tbsp ghee
- ¼ cup roasted hazelnuts
- A pinch of cayenne pepper

Directions

1. Preheat your oven to 425 °F. Line a baking dish with waxed paper.

2. Melt the ghee and brush it over the fish. In a food processor, combine the rest of the ingredients. Coat the cod with the hazelnut mixture. Place in the oven and bake for about 15 minutes.

Per serving: Calories 467, Fat: 31g, Net Carbs: 2.8g, Protein: 40g

Beef Burgers with Roasted Brussels Sprouts

Prep + Cook Time: 30 minutes | Serves: 4

Ingredients

For the beef burgers

- 1 pound ground beef
- 1 egg
- ½ onion, chopped
- 1 tsp salt
- ½ tsp ground black pepper
- 1 tsp dried thyme
- 2 oz butter

For the fried Brussels sprouts

- 1 ½ lb Brussels sprouts, halved
- 3 oz butter
- 1 tsp salt
- ½ tsp ground black pepper

Directions

1. Combine the burger ingredients in a mixing bowl.

2. Create patties from the mixture. Set a large pan over medium-high heat, warm butter, and fry the patties until cooked completely. Place on a plate and cover with aluminium foil to keep warm. Fry brussels sprouts in butter, season to your preference, then set to a bowl.

3. Plate the burgers and brussels sprouts and serve.

Per serving: Calories: 443, Fat: 25g, Net Carbs: 5.8g, Protein: 31g

Sushi Rolls with Prawn and Cucumber

Prep + Cook Time: 10 minutes | Serves: 5

Ingredients

- 2 cups prawns, cooked and chopped
- 1 tbsp sriracha sauce
- ¼ cucumber, julienned
- 5 hand roll nori sheets
- ¼ cup mayonnaise

Directions

1. Combine prawns, mayonnaise, and sriracha in a bowl. Lay out a single nori sheet on a flat surface and spread about 1/5 of the prawn mixture. Roll the nori sheet as desired. Repeat with the other ingredients.

Per serving: Calories 216, Fat: 10g, Net Carbs: 1g, Protein: 18.7g

Baked Cheese and Cauliflower

Prep + Cook Time: 21 minutes | Serves: 4

Ingredients

- 2 heads cauliflower, cut into florets
- ¼ cup butter, cubed
- 2 tbsp melted butter
- 1 white onion, chopped
- Salt and black pepper to taste
- ¼ almond milk
- ½ cup almond flour
- 1 ½ cups grated Colby cheese
- Water for sprinkling

Directions

1. Preheat oven to 350°F and put the cauli florets in a large microwave-safe bowl. Sprinkle with water, and steam in the microwave for 4 to 5 minutes.

2. Melt the ¼ cup of butter in a saucepan over medium heat and sauté the onions for 3 minutes. Add the cauliflower, season with salt and black pepper and mix in almond milk. Simmer for 3 minutes.

3. Mix the remaining melted butter with almond flour. Stir into the cauliflower as well as half of the cheese. Sprinkle the top with the remaining cheese and bake for 10 minutes until the cheese has melted and golden brown on the top. Plate the bake and serve with arugula salad.

Per serving: Calories 215, Fat 15g, Net Carbs 4g, Protein 12g

Chapter 5: Dinner

Provolone Chicken Spinach Bake

Prep + Cook Time: 45 minutes | Serves: 6

Ingredients

- 6 chicken breasts, skinless and boneless
- 1 tsp mixed spice seasoning
- Pink salt and black pepper to season
- 2 loose cups baby spinach
- 3 tsp olive oil
- 4 oz cream cheese, cubed
- 1 ¼ cups provolone cheese, shredded
- 4 tbsp water

Directions

1. Preheat oven to 370°F.
2. Season chicken with spice mix, salt, and black pepper. Pat with your hands to have the seasoning stick on the chicken. Put in the casserole dish and layer spinach over the chicken.
3. Mix the oil with cream cheese, provolone cheese, salt, and black pepper and stir in water a tablespoon at a time. Pour the mixture over the chicken and cover the pot with aluminium foil.
4. Bake for 20 minutes, remove foil and continue cooking for 15 minutes until a nice golden brown color is formed on top. Take out and allow sitting for 5 minutes.
5. Serve warm with braised asparagus.

Per serving: Calories 340, Fat 30.2g, Net Carbs 3.1g, Protein 15g

Prosciutto-Wrapped Chicken with Asparagus

Prep + Cook Time: 48 minutes | Serves: 4

Ingredients

- 6 chicken breasts
- 8 prosciutto slices
- 4 tbsp olive oil
- 1 lb asparagus spears
- Salt and black pepper to taste
- 2 tbsp fresh lemon juice
- Manchego cheese for topping

Directions

1. Preheat the oven to 400°F.

2. Season chicken breasts with salt and black pepper, and wrap 2 prosciutto slices around each chicken breast. Arrange on a baking sheet that is lined with parchment paper, drizzle with oil and bake for 25-30 minutes until bacon is brown and crispy.

3. Preheat your grill on high heat.

4. Brush the asparagus spears with olive oil and season with salt. Grill for 8-10 minutes, frequently turning until slightly charred. Remove to a plate and drizzle with lemon juice. Grate over Manchego cheese so that it melts a little on contact with the hot asparagus and forms a cheesy dressing.

Per serving: Calories 468, Fat 38g, Net Carbs 2g, Protein 26g

Paleo Coconut Flour Chicken Nuggets

Prep + Cook Time: 25 minutes | Serves: 2

Ingredients

- ½ cup coconut flour
- 1 egg
- 2 tbsp garlic powder
- 2 chicken breasts, cubed
- Salt and black pepper, to taste
- ½ cup butter

Directions

1. Using a bowl, combine salt, garlic powder, flour, and pepper, and stir. In a separate bowl, beat the egg. Add the chicken breast cubes in egg mixture, then in the flour mixture.

2. Set a pan over medium-high heat and warm butter, add in the chicken nuggets, and cook for 6 minutes on each side. Remove to paper towels, drain the excess grease and serve.

Per serving: Calories 417, Fat 37g, Net Carbs 4.3g, Protein 35g

Pickled Peppers and Grilled Beef Salad with Feta

Prep + Cook Time: 15 minutes | Serves: 4

Ingredients

- 1 lb skirt steak, sliced
- Salt and black pepper to season
- 1 tsp olive oil
- 4 radishes, sliced
- 1 ½ cups mixed salad greens
- 3 chopped pickled peppers
- 2 tbsp red wine vinaigrette
- ½ cup feta cheese, crumbled

Directions

1. Brush the steaks with olive oil and season with salt and pepper on both sides.

2. Heat frying pan over high heat and cook the steaks on each side to the desired doneness, for about 5-6 minutes.

3. Remove to a bowl, cover and leave to rest while you make the salad.

4. Mix the salad greens, radishes, pickled peppers, and vinaigrette in a salad bowl.

5. Add the beef and sprinkle with cheese. Serve the salad with roasted parsnips.

Per serving: Calories 315, Fat 26g, Net Carbs 2g, Protein 18g

Baked Chicken Skewers with Rutabaga Fries

Prep + Cook Time: 60 minutes | Serves: 4

Ingredients

- 2 chicken breasts
- ½ tsp salt
- ¼ tsp ground black pepper
- 2 tbsp olive oil
- ¼ cup chicken broth

For the fries

- 1lb rutabaga
- 2 tbsp olive oil
- ½ tsp salt
- ¼ tsp ground black pepper

Directions

1. Set an oven to 400°F. Grease and line a baking sheet. In a large bowl, mix oil, spices and the chicken; set in the fridge for 10 minutes while covered. Peel and chop rutabaga to form fry shapes and place into a separate bowl. Apply oil to coat and add pepper and salt for seasoning. Arrange to the baking tray in an even layer and bake for 10 minutes.

2. Take the chicken from the refrigerator and thread onto the skewers. Place over the rutabaga, pour in the chicken broth, then set in the oven for 30 minutes. Serve with lemon wedges.

Per serving: Calories: 579, Fat: 53g, Net Carbs: 6g, Protein: 39g

Tuna Salad Pickle Boats

Prep + Cook Time: 40 minutes | Serves: 12

Ingredients

- 18 ounces canned and drained tuna
- 6 large dill pickles
- ¼ tsp garlic powder
- ¼ cup sugar-free mayonnaise
- 1 tsp onion powder

Directions

1. Combine the mayonnaise, tuna, onion powder, and garlic powder in a bowl. Cut the pickles in half lengthwise.

2. Top each half with tuna mixture. Place in the fridge for 30 minutes before serving.

Per serving: Calories 118, Fat: 10g, Net Carbs: 1.5g, Protein: 11g

Turkey with Avocado Sauce

Prep + Cook Time: 22 minutes | Serves: 4

Ingredients

For the sauce

- 1 avocado, pitted
- ½ cup mayonnaise
- Salt to taste

For the turkey

- 3 tbsp ghee
- 4 turkey breasts
- Salt and black pepper to taste
- 1 cup chopped cilantro leaves
- ½ cup chicken broth

Directions

1. Spoon the avocado, mayonnaise, and salt into a small food processor and puree until smooth sauce is derived. Adjust taste with salt as desired.

2. Pour sauce into a jar and refrigerate while you make the turkey.

3. Melt ghee in a large skillet, season turkey with salt and black pepper and fry for 4 minutes on each side to golden brown. Remove turkey to a plate.

4. Pour the broth in the same skillet and add the cilantro. Bring to simmer covered for 3 minutes and add the turkey. Cover and cook on low heat for 5 minutes until liquid has reduced and turkey is fragrant. Dish turkey only into serving plates and spoon the mayo-avocado sauce over.

Per serving: Calories 398, Fat 32g, Net Carbs 4g, Protein 24g

Smothered Chicken Breasts with Bacon

Prep + Cook Time: 25 minutes | Serves: 6

Ingredients

- 7 strips bacon, chopped
- 3 chicken breasts, halved
- Salt and black pepper to taste
- 5 sprigs fresh thyme + extra to garnish
- ¼ cup chicken broth
- ½ cup heavy cream

Directions

1. Cook bacon in a large skillet on medium heat for 5 minutes to be crispy. Remove with a slotted spoon onto a paper towel-lined plate to soak up excess fat.

2. Season chicken breasts with salt and black pepper and brown in the bacon fat for 4 minutes on each side. Remove to the bacon plate.

3. Stir in the thyme, chicken broth, and heavy cream and simmer for 5 minutes. Season with salt and black pepper.

4. Return the chicken and bacon, and cook further for another 2 minutes. Serve chicken and a generous ladle of sauce with cauli mash. Garnish with thyme leaves.

Per serving: Calories 435, Fat 37g, Net Carbs 3g, Protein 22g

Tomato Basil Stuffed Chicken Breasts

Prep + Cook Time: 45 minutes | Serves: 6

Ingredients

- 4 ounces cream cheese
- 3 oz provolone cheese slices
- 10 ounces spinach
- ½ cup mozzarella cheese, shredded
- 1 tbsp olive oil
- 1 cup tomato basil sauce
- 3 whole chicken breasts

Directions

1. Preheat your oven to 400°F. Combine the cream cheese, provolone cheese slices, and spinach in the microwave.

2. Cut the chicken with the knife a couple of times horizontally. Stuff with the filling. Brush the top with olive oil. Place on a lined baking dish and in the oven. Bake in the oven for 25 minutes.

3. Pour the sauce over and top with mozzarella cheese. Return to oven and cook for 5 minutes.

Per serving: Calories 338, Fat: 28g, Net Carbs: 2.5g, Protein: 37g

Chicken with Tomato and Zucchini

Prep + Cook Time: 45 minutes | Serves: 4

Ingredients

- 2 tbsp ghee
- 1 lb chicken thighs
- Pink salt and black pepper to taste
- 2 cloves garlic, minced
- 1 (14 oz) can whole tomatoes
- 1 zucchini, diced
- 10 fresh basil leaves, chopped + extra to garnish

Directions

1. Melt ghee in a saucepan over medium heat, season the chicken with salt and black pepper, and fry for 4 minutes on each side until golden brown. Remove chicken onto a plate.

2. Sauté the garlic in the ghee for 2 minutes, pour in the tomatoes, and cook covered for 8 minutes.

3. Add in the zucchini and basil. Cook for 4 minutes. Season the sauce with salt and black pepper, stir and add the chicken. Coat with sauce and simmer for 3 minutes.

4. Serve chicken with sauce on a bed of squash pasta. Garnish with extra basil.

Per serving: Calories 468, Fat 39.5g, Net Carbs 2g, Protein 26g

Granberry Glazed Chili Chicken with Green Onions

Prep + Cook Time: 50 minutes | Serves: 6

Ingredients

- 4 green onions, chopped diagonally
- 2 lb chicken wings
- 4 tbsp unsweetened cranberry puree
- 2 tbsp olive oil
- Salt to taste
- Chili sauce to taste
- Juice from 1 lime

Directions

1. Preheat the oven (broiler side) to 400°F. Then, in a bowl, mix the cranberry puree, olive oil, salt, sweet chili sauce, and lime juice. After, add in the wings and toss to coat.

2. Place the chicken under the broiler, and cook for 45 minutes, turning once halfway.

3. Remove the chicken after and serve warm with a cranberry puree and cheese dipping sauce.

4. Top with green onions to serve.

Per serving: Calories 152, Fat 8.5g, Net Carbs 1.6g, Protein 17.6g

Paprika Chicken and Bacon Stew

Prep + Cook Time: 40 minutes | Serves: 3

Ingredients

- 8 bacon strips, chopped
- ¼ cup Dijon mustard
- Salt and black pepper, to taste
- 1 onion, chopped
- 1 tbsp olive oil
- 1 ½ cups chicken stock
- 3 chicken breasts, skinless and boneless
- ¼ tsp sweet paprika

Directions

1. Using a bowl, combine the pepper, salt, and mustard. Sprinkle this on chicken breasts and massage. Set a pan over medium-high heat, stir in the bacon, cook until it browns, and remove to a plate.

2. Place oil in the same pan and heat over medium-high heat, add in the chicken breasts, cook for each side for 2 minutes and set aside.

3. Place in the stock, and bring to a simmer. Stir in pepper, pancetta, salt, and onions. Return the chicken to the pan as well, stir gently, and simmer for 20 minutes over medium heat, turning the meat halfway through.

4. Split the chicken on serving plates, sprinkle the sauce over it to serve.

Per serving: Calories 313, Fat 18g, Net Carbs 3g, Protein 26g

Grilled Garlic Chicken with Steamed Cauliflower

Prep + Cook Time: 17 minutes | Serves: 6

Ingredients

- 3 tbsp smoked paprika
- Salt and black pepper to taste
- 2 tsp garlic powder
- 1 tbsp olive oil
- 6 chicken breasts
- 1 head cauliflower, cut into florets

Directions

1. Place the cauliflower florets onto the steamer basket over boiling water and steam for approximately 8 minutes or until crisp-tender; set aside. Grease grill grate with cooking spray and preheat to 400°F.

2. Combine paprika, salt, black pepper, and garlic powder in a bowl. Brush chicken with olive oil and sprinkle spice mixture over and massage with hands.

3. Grill chicken for 7 minutes per side until well-cooked, and plate. Serve warm with steamed cauliflower.

Per serving: Calories 422, Fat 35.3g, Net Carbs 2g, Protein 26g

Yellow Squash Duck Breasts Stew

Prep + Cook Time: 20 minutes | Serves: 2

Ingredients

- 2 duck breasts, skin on and sliced
- 2 yellow squash, sliced
- 1 tbsp coconut oil
- 1 green onion bunch, chopped
- 1 carrot, chopped
- 2 green bell peppers, seeded and chopped
- Salt and ground black pepper, to taste

Directions

1. Set a pan over medium-high heat and warm oil, stir in the green onions, and cook for 2 minutes.
2. Place in the yellow squash, bell peppers, pepper, salt, and carrot, and cook for 10 minutes.
3. Set another pan over medium-high heat, add in duck slices and cook each side for 3 minutes.
4. Pour the mixture into the vegetable pan. Cook for 3 minutes.
5. Set in bowls and enjoy.

Per serving: Calories 433, Fat 21g, Net Carbs 8g, Protein 53g

Acorn Squash Chicken Traybake

Prep + Cook Time: 60 minutes | Serves: 4

Ingredients

- 2 lb chicken thighs
- 1 lb acorn squash, cubed
- ½ cup black olives, pitted
- ¼ cup olive oil
- 5 garlic cloves, sliced
- 1 tbsp dried oregano
- Salt and black pepper, to taste

Directions

1. Set oven to 400°F and grease a baking dish. Place in the chicken with the skin down. Set the garlic, olives and acorn squash around the chicken then drizzle with oil.

2. Spread pepper, salt, and thyme over the mixture then add into the oven. Cook for 45 minutes.

Per serving: Calories: 411, Fat: 15g, Net Carbs: 5.5g, Protein: 31g

Cheese Muffins with Ajillo Mushrooms

Prep + Cook Time: 45 minutes | Serves: 6

Ingredients

- 1 ½ cups double cream
- 5 ounces mascarpone cheese
- 3 eggs, beaten
- Salt and black pepper, to taste
- 1 tbsp butter, softened
- 2 cups mushrooms, chopped
- 2 garlic cloves, minced

Directions

1. Preheat the oven to 320°F. Insert 6 ramekins into a large pan. Add in boiling water up to 1-inch depth. In a pan, over medium heat, warm double cream.

2. Set heat to a simmer; stir in mascarpone cheese and cook until melted.

3. Set the beaten eggs in a bowl and place in 3 tablespoons of the hot cream mixture; combine well. Place the mixture back to the pan with hot cream/cheese mixture.

4. Sprinkle with pepper and salt. Ladle the mixture into ramekins. Bake for 40 minutes.

5. Melt butter in a pan over medium heat. Add garlic and mushrooms, season with salt and pepper and sauté for 5-6 minutes until tender and translucent.

6. Spread the ajillo mushrooms on top of each cooled muffin to serve.

Per serving: Calories 263, Fat: 22.4g, Net Carbs: 6.1g, Protein: 10g

Cheesy Chicken Tenders

Prep + Cook Time: 40 minutes | Serves: 4

Ingredients

- 2 eggs
- 3 tbsp butter, melted
- 3 cups Monterey Jack cheese, crushed
- ½ cup pork rinds, crushed
- 1 lb chicken tenders
- Salt to taste

Directions

1. Preheat oven to 350°F and line a baking sheet with parchment paper. Whisk the eggs with the butter in one bowl and mix the cheese and pork rinds in another bowl.

2. Season chicken with salt, dip in egg mixture, and coat in cheddar mixture. Place on baking sheet, cover with aluminium foil and bake for 25 minutes. Remove foil and bake further for 12 minutes to golden brown. Serve chicken with mustard dip.

Per serving: Calories 507, Fat 54g, Net Carbs 1.3g, Protein 42g

Baked Cheese Chicken with Acorn Squash

Prep + Cook Time: 1 hour 15 minutes | Serves: 6

Ingredients

- 6 chicken breasts, skinless and boneless
- 1 lb acorn squash, peeled and sliced
- Salt and ground black pepper, to taste
- 1 cup blue cheese, crumbled

Directions

1. Take cooking oil and spray on a baking dish, add in chicken breasts, pepper, squash, and salt and drizzle with olive.

2. Transfer to the oven set at 420°F, and bake for 1 hour. Scatter blue cheese, and bake for 15 minutes. Remove to a serving plate and enjoy.

Per serving: Calories 235, Fat 16g, Net Carbs 5g, Protein 12g

Roasted Chicken with Yogurt Scallions Sauce

Prep + Cook Time: 35 minutes | Serves: 4

Ingredients

- 2 tbsp butter
- 4 scallions, chopped
- 4 chicken breasts, skinless and boneless
- Salt and black pepper, to taste
- 6 ounces plain yogurt
- 2 tbsp fresh dill, chopped

Directions

1. Heat a pan with the butter over medium-high heat, add in the chicken, season with pepper and salt, and fry for 2-3 per side until golden. Transfer to a baking dish and cook in the oven for 15 minutes at 390°F, until no longer pink.

2. To the pan add scallions, and cook for 2 minutes. Pour in the plain yogurt, warm through without boil. Slice the chicken and serve on a platter with green sauce.

Per serving: Calories 236, Fat 9g, Net Carbs 2.3g, Protein 18g

Coconut Smoothie with Berries

Prep + Cook Time: 5 minutes | Serves: 4

Ingredients

- ½ cup water
- 1 ½ cups coconut milk
- 1 cup fresh blackberries
- 4 cup fresh blueberries
- ¼ tsp vanilla extract
- 1 tbsp vegan protein powder

Directions

1. Using a blender, combine all the ingredients and blend well until you attain a uniform and creamy consistency. Divide in glasses and serve!

Per serving: Calories 247; Fat: 21.7g, Net Carbs: 14.9g, Protein: 2.6g

Tuna Stuffed Avocado

Prep + Cook Time: 20 minutes | Serves: 4

Ingredients

- 2 avocados, halved and pitted
- 4 ounces Colby Jack cheese, grated
- 2 ounces canned tuna, flaked
- 2 tbsp chives, chopped
- Salt and black pepper, to taste
- ½ cup curly endive, chopped

Directions

1. Set oven to 360°F. Set avocado halves in an ovenproof dish. Using a mixing bowl, mix colby jack cheese, chives, pepper, salt, and tuna. Stuff the cheese/tuna mixture in avocado halves.

2. Bake for 15 minutes or until the top is golden brown. Sprinkle with fresh cilantro and serve with curly endive for garnish.

Per serving: Calories: 286; Fat 23.9g, Net Carbs 9g, Protein 11.2g

Stuffed Avocado with Plain Yogurt and Crabmeat

Prep + Cook Time: 25 minutes | Serves: 4

Ingredients

- 1 tsp olive oil
- 1 cup crabmeat
- 2 avocados, halved and pitted
- 3 oz plain yogurt, strained overnight in a cheesecloth
- ¼ cup almonds, chopped
- 1 tsp smoked paprika

Directions

1. Set oven to 425°F. Grease oil on a baking pan.

2. In a bowl, mix crabmeat with plain yogurt. To the avocado halves, place in almonds and crabmeat/cheese mixture and bake for 18 minutes. Decorate with paprika to serve.

Per serving: Calories 264, Fat: 24.4g, Net Carbs: 11g, Protein: 3.7g

Prosciutto Eggplant Boats

Prep + Cook Time: 35 minutes | Serves: 3

Ingredients

- 3 eggplants, cut into halves
- 1 tbsp deli mustard
- 2 prosciutto slices, chopped
- 6 eggs
- Salt, to taste + ¼ tsp black pepper
- ¼ tsp dried parsley

Directions

1. Scoop flesh from eggplant halves to make shells; set the eggplant boats on a greased baking pan. Spread mustard on the bottom of every eggplant half. Split the prosciutto among eggplant boats.

2. Crack an egg in each half, sprinkle with parsley, pepper, and salt. Set oven at 400°F and bake for 30 minutes or until boats become tender.

Per serving: Calories 506; Fat 41g, Net Carbs 4.5g, Protein 27.5g

Keto Pizza Dough

Prep + Cook Time: 8 minutes | Serves: 8

Ingredients

- 3 cups almond flour
- 3 tbsp ghee
- ¼ tsp salt
- 3 large eggs

Directions

1. Preheat the oven to 350°F and in a bowl, mix the almond flour, ghee, salt, and eggs until a dough forms. Mold the dough into a ball and place in between two wide parchment papers on a flat surface.

2. Use a rolling pin to roll it out into a circle of a quarter-inch thickness. Slide the pizza dough into the pizza pan and remove the parchment papers. Bake the dough for 20 minutes. Garnish of your choice.

Per serving: Calories 151; Fat: 13.1g, Net Carbs: 2.7g, Protein: 7.3g

Broccoli Gratin with Gorgonzola Cheese

Prep + Cook Time: 15 minutes | Serves: 4

Ingredients

- 1 ½ pounds broccoli, broken into florets
- 2 tbsp olive oil, divided
- 1 tsp crushed garlic
- 1 rosemary sprig, chopped
- 1 thyme sprig, chopped
- 2 cups gorgonzola cheese, crumbled
- Black pepper to taste

Directions

1. Place salted water in a deep pan and set over medium heat. Add in broccoli and boil for 8 minutes. Remove the cooked florets to a casserole dish.

2. In a food processor, pulse ½ of the broccoli. Place in 1 tablespoon of oil and 1 cup of the cooking liquid. Do the same with the remaining water, broccoli, and 1 tablespoon of olive oil. Stir in the remaining ingredients and serve.

Per serving: Calories 230, Fat: 17.7g, Net Carbs: 7.2g, Protein: 11.9g

Turnip Chips with Avocado Dip

Prep + Cook Time: 20 minutes | Serves: 6

Ingredients

- 2 avocados, pitted
- 2 tsp lime juice
- Salt and black pepper, to taste
- 2 garlic cloves, minced
- 2 tbsp olive oil

For turnip chips

- 1 ½ pounds turnips, sliced
- 1 tbsp olive oil
- ½ tsp onion powder
- ½ tsp garlic powder
- Salt to taste

Directions

1. Use a fork to mash avocado pulp. Stir in fresh lime juice, pepper, 2 tbsp of olive oil, garlic, and salt until well combined. Remove to a bowl and set the oven to 300 °F. Grease a baking sheet with spray.

2. Set turnip slices on the baking sheet; toss with garlic powder, 1 tbps of olive oil, and salt. Bake for 15 minutes until slices become dry. Serve alongside well-chilled avocado dip.

Per serving: Calories 269; Fat: 26.7g, Net Carbs: 9.4g, Protein: 2.3g

Herby Mushrooms Stroganoff

Prep + Cook Time: 15 minutes | Serves: 4

Ingredients

- 3 tbsp butter
- 1 white onion, chopped
- 4 cups white mushrooms, cubed
- 2 cups water
- ½ cup heavy cream
- ½ cup grated Pecorino Romano cheese
- 1 ½ tbsp dried mixed herbs
- Salt and black pepper to taste

Directions

1. Melt the butter in a saucepan over medium heat, sauté the onion for 3 minutes until soft.

2. Stir in the mushrooms and cook until tender, about 3 minutes.

3. Add the water, mix, and bring to boil for 4 minutes until the water reduces slightly.

4. Pour in the heavy cream and pecorino romano cheese. Stir to melt the cheese. Also, mix in the dried herbs. Season with salt and pepper, simmer for 40 seconds and turn the heat off.

5. Ladle stroganoff over a bed of spaghetti squash and serve.

Per serving: Calories 284, Fat 28g, Net Carbs 1,5g, Protein 8g

Hazelnut Tofu Stir-Fry

Prep + Cook Time: 15 minutes | Serves: 4

Ingredients

- 1 tbsp olive oil
- 1 (8 oz) block firm tofu, cubed
- 1 tbsp tomato paste with garlic and onion
- 1 tbsp balsamic vinegar
- Pink salt and black pepper to taste
- ½ tsp mixed dried herbs
- 1 cup chopped raw hazelnuts

Directions

1. Heat the oil in a skillet over medium heat and cook the tofu for 3 minutes while stirring to brown.

2. Mix the tomato paste with the vinegar and add to the tofu. Stir, season with salt and black pepper, and cook for another 4 minutes.

3. Add the herbs and hazelnuts. Stir and cook on low heat for 3 minutes to be fragrant. Spoon to a side of squash mash and a sweet berry sauce to serve.

Per serving: Calories 320, Fat 24g, Net Carbs 4g, Protein 18g

Tomato Bites with Vegan Cheese Topping

Prep + Cook Time: 15 minutes | Serves: 6

Ingredients

- 2 spring onions, chopped
- 5 tomatoes, sliced
- ¼ cup olive oil
- 1 tbsp seasoning mix

For vegan cheese

- ½ cup pepitas seeds
- 1 tbsp nutritional yeast
- Salt and black pepper, to taste
- 1 tsp garlic puree

Directions

1. Over the sliced tomatoes, drizzle olive oil. Set oven to 200°F.

2. In a food processor, add all vegan cheese ingredients and pulse until the desired consistency is attained. Combine vegan cheese and seasoning mixture. Toss in seasoned tomato slices to coat.

3. Set the tomato slices on the prepared baking pan and bake for 10 minutes.

4. Top with spring onions to serve.

Per serving: Calories 161; Fat: 14g, Net Carbs: 7.2g, Protein: 4.6g

Spinach Cheese Stuffed Flank Steak Rolls

Prep + Cook Time: 42 minutes | Serves: 6

Ingredients

- 1 ½ lb flank steak
- Salt and black pepper to season
- 1 cup ricotta cheese, crumbled
- ½ loose cup baby spinach
- 1 jalapeño pepper, chopped
- ¼ cup chopped basil leaves

Directions

1. Preheat oven to 400°F and grease a baking sheet with cooking spray.

2. Wrap the steak in plastic wrap, place on a flat surface, and gently run a rolling pin over to flatten. Take off the wraps.

3. Sprinkle with half of the ricotta cheese, top with spinach, jalapeño, basil leaves, and the remaining cheese. Roll the steak over on the stuffing and secure with toothpicks.

4. Place in the greased baking sheet and cook for 30 minutes, flipping once until nicely browned on the outside and the cheese melted within.

5. Cool for 3 minutes, slice into pinwheels and serve with thyme sautéed mixed veggies.

Per serving: Calories 490, Fat 41g, Net Carbs 2g, Protein 28g

Sesame Cauliflower Dip

Prep + Cook Time: 10 minutes | Serves: 4

Ingredients

- ¾ pound cauliflower, cut into florets
- ¼ cup olive oil
- Salt and black pepper, to taste
- 1 garlic clove, smashed
- 1 tbsp sesame paste
- 1 tbsp fresh lemon juice
- ½ tsp garam masala

Directions

1. Steam cauliflower until tender for 7 minutes in.

2. Transfer to a blender and pulse until you attain a rice-like consistency.

3. Place in Garam Masala, oil, black paper, fresh lemon juice, garlic, salt, and sesame paste. Blend the mixture until well combined.

4. Decorate with some additional olive oil and serve. Otherwise, refrigerate until ready to use.

Per serving: Calories 100; Fat: 8.2g, Net Carbs: 4.7g, Protein: 3.7g

Beef Broccoli Curry

Prep + Cook Time: 26 minutes | Serves: 6

Ingredients

- 1 tbsp olive oil
- 1 ½ lb ground beef
- 1 tbsp ginger-garlic paste
- 1 tsp garam masala
- 1 (7 oz) can whole tomatoes
- 1 head broccoli, cut into florets
- Salt and chili pepper to taste
- ¼ cup water

Directions

1. Heat oil in a saucepan over medium heat, add the beef, ginger-garlic paste and season with garam masala. Cook for 5 minutes while breaking any lumps. Stir in the tomatoes and broccoli, season with salt and chili pepper, and cook covered for 6 minutes.

2. Add the water and bring to a boil over medium heat for 10 minutes or until the water has reduced by half. Adjust taste with salt. Spoon the curry into serving bowls and serve with shirataki rice.

Per serving: Calories 374, Fat 33g, Net Carbs 2g, Protein 22g

Polish Beef Tripe

Prep + Cook Time: 30 minutes + cooling time | Serves: 6

Ingredients

- 1 ½ lb beef tripe
- 4 cups buttermilk
- Salt and black pepper to taste
- 1 parsnip, chopped
- 2 tsp marjoram
- 3 tbsp butter
- 2 large onions, sliced
- 3 tomatoes, diced

Directions

1. Put tripe in a bowl and cover with buttermilk. Refrigerate for 3 hours to extract bitterness and gamey taste. Remove from buttermilk, pat dry with paper towel, and season with salt and black pepper.

2. Heat 2 tablespoons of butter in a skillet over medium heat and brown the tripe on both sides for 6 minutes in total. Remove and set aside.

3. Add the remaining oil and sauté the onions for 3 minutes until soft. Include the tomatoes and parsnip, and cook for 15 minutes. Pour in a few tablespoons of water if necessary. Put the tripe in the sauce and cook for 3 minutes. Serve very hot.

Per serving: Calories 342, Fat 27g, Net Carbs 1g, Protein 22g

Spinach with Garlic Thyme

Prep + Cook Time: 25 minutes | Serves: 4

Ingredients

- 2 pound spinach, chopped
- 2 tbsp almond oil
- 1 tsp garlic, minced
- ½ tsp thyme
- ½ tsp red pepper flakes, crushed
- Salt and black pepper, to the taste

Directions

1. Add spinach in a pot containing salted water and cook for 10 minutes over medium heat. Drain and set aside.

2. Place a sauté pan over medium-high heat and warm the oil.

3. Add in garlic and cook until soft. Stir in the spinach, red pepper, black pepper, salt, and thyme and ensure they are heated through. Add more seasonings if needed and serve warm with cauli rice.

Per serving: Calories 118; Fat: 7g, Net Carbs: 13.4g, Protein: 2.9g

Beef with Broccoli Rice and Eggs

Prep + Cook Time: 22 minutes | Serves: 4

Ingredients

- 2 cups cauli rice
- 3 cups frozen mixed vegetables
- 3 tbsp butter
- 1 lb sirloin steak, sliced
- Salt and black pepper to taste
- 4 fresh eggs
- Hot sauce (sugar-free) for topping

Directions

1. Mix the cauli rice and mixed vegetables in a bowl, sprinkle with a little water, and steam in the microwave for 1 minute to be tender. Share into 4 serving bowls.

2. Melt the butter in a skillet, season the beef with salt and pepper, and brown for 5 minutes on each side. Use a perforated spoon to ladle the meat onto the vegetables.

3. Wipe out the skillet and return to medium heat, crack in an egg, season with salt and pepper and cook until the egg white has set, but the yolk is still runny 3 minutes.

4. Remove egg onto the vegetable bowl and fry the remaining 3 eggs. Add to the other bowls.

5. Drizzle the beef bowls with hot sauce and serve.

Per serving: Calories 320, Fat 26g, Net Carbs 4g, Protein 15g

Tasty Beef Cheeseburgers

Prep + Cook Time: 15 minutes | Serves: 4

Ingredients

- 1 lb ground beef
- 1 tsp dried parsley
- ½ tsp sugar-free Worcestershire sauce
- Salt and black pepper to taste
- 1 cup feta cheese, shredded
- 4 low carb buns, halved

Directions

1. Preheat a grill to 400°F and grease the grate with cooking spray.

2. Mix the beef, parsley, Worcestershire sauce, salt, and black pepper with your hands until evenly combined.

3. Make medium sized patties out of the mixture, about 4 patties. Cook on the grill for 7 minutes one side to be cooked through and no longer pink.

4. Flip the patties and top with cheese. Cook for another 7 minutes to be well done while the cheese melts onto the meat.

5. Remove the patties and sandwich into two halves of a bun each.

6. Serve with a tomato dipping sauce and zucchini fries.

Per serving: Calories 386, Fat 32g, Net Carbs 2g, Protein 21g

Burritos with Avocado Greek Yogurt Filling

Prep + Cook Time: 5 minutes | Serves: 4

Ingredients

- 2 cups cauli rice
- Water for sprinkling
- 6 zero carb flatbread
- 2 cups Greek yogurt
- 1 ½ cups tomato herb salsa
- 2 avocados, peeled, pitted, sliced

Directions

1. Pour the cauli rice in a bowl, sprinkle with water, and soften in the microwave for 2 minutes.

2. On flatbread, spread the Greek yogurt all over and distribute the salsa on top. Top with cauli rice and scatter the avocado evenly on top. Fold and tuck the burritos and cut into two.

Per serving: Calories 303, Fat 25g, Net Carbs 6g, Protein 8g

Baked Spicy Cauliflower and Peppers

Prep + Cook Time: 35 minutes | Serves: 4

Ingredients

- 1 pound cauliflower, cut into florets
- 1 yellow bell pepper, halved
- 1 red bell pepper, halved
- ¼ cup olive oil
- Salt and black pepper, to taste
- ½ tsp cayenne pepper
- 1 tsp curry powder

Directions

1. Set oven to 425 °F. Line a parchment paper to a large baking sheet. Sprinkle olive oil to the peppers and cauliflower alongside curry powder, black pepper, salt, and cayenne pepper.

2. Set the vegetables on the baking sheet. Roast for 30 minutes as you toss in intervals until they start to brown.

3. Serve alongside mushroom pate or homemade tomato dip!

Per serving: Calories 166; Fat: 13.9g, Net Carbs: 7.4g, Protein: 3g

Beef Steak Fajitas

Prep + Cook Time: 7 minutes | Serves: 4

Ingredients

- 2 lb flank steak, cut in halves
- 2 tbsp Adobo seasoning
- Salt to taste
- 2 tbsp olive oil
- 2 large white onion, chopped
- 1 cup sliced mixed bell peppers, chopped
- 12 low carb tortillas

Directions

1. Season the steak with adobo and marinate in the fridge for one hour.

2. Preheat grill to 425°F and cook steak for 6 minutes on each side, flipping once until lightly browned.

3. Remove from heat and wrap in foil and let sit for 10 minutes. This allows the meat to cook in its heat for a few more minutes before slicing.

4. Heat the olive oil in a skillet over medium heat and sauté the onion and bell peppers for 5 minutes or until soft.

5. Cut steak against the grain into strips and share on the tortillas.

6. Top with vegetables and serve with guacamole.

Per serving: Calories 348, Fat 25g, Net Carbs 5g, Protein 18g

Veal Chops with Raspberry Sauce

Prep + Cook Time: 17 minutes | Serves: 4

Ingredients

- 1 tbsp olive oil + extra for brushing
- 2 lb veal chops
- Salt and black pepper to taste
- 2 cups raspberries
- ¼ cup water
- 1 ½ tbsp Italian Herb mix
- 3 tbsp balsamic vinegar
- 2 tsp sugar-free Worcestershire sauce

Directions

1. Heat oil in a skillet over medium heat, season the veal with salt and black pepper and cook for 5 minutes on each side. Put on serving plates and reserve the pork drippings.
2. Mash the raspberries with a fork in a bowl until jam-like.
3. Pour into a saucepan, add the water, and herb mix. Bring to boil on low heat for 4 minutes. Stir in veal drippings, vinegar, and Worcestershire sauce. Simmer for 1 minute.
4. Spoon sauce over the veal chops and serve with braised rapini.

Per serving: Calories 413, Fat 32.5g, Net Carbs 1.1g, Protein 26.3g

Baked Stuffed Avocados

Prep + Cook Time: 20 minutes | Serves: 4

Ingredients

- 3 avocados, halved and pitted, skin on
- ½ cup mozzarella cheese, shredded
- ½ cup Swiss cheese, grated
- 2 eggs, beaten
- Salt and black pepper, to taste
- 1 tbsp fresh basil, chopped

Directions

1. Set oven to 360°F. Lay the avocado halves in an ovenproof dish. Using a mixing dish, mix both types of cheeses, pepper, eggs, and salt.

2. Split the mixture equally into the avocado halves.

3. Bake thoroughly for 15 to 17 minutes. Decorate with fresh basil before serving.

Per serving: Calories 342; Fat: 30.4g, Net Carbs: 7.5g, Protein: 11.1g

Cheese and Beef Bake

Prep + Cook Time: 30 minutes | Serves: 6

Ingredients

- 2 lb ground beef
- Salt and black pepper to taste
- 1 cup cauli rice
- 2 cups chopped cabbage
- 14 oz can diced tomatoes
- ¼ cup water
- 1 cup shredded Gouda cheese

Directions

1. Preheat oven to 370°F and grease a baking dish with cooking spray. Put beef in a pot and season with salt and black pepper and cook over medium heat for 6 minutes until no longer pink. Drain grease.

2. Add cauli rice, cabbage, tomatoes, and water. Stir and bring to boil covered for 5 minutes to thicken the sauce. Adjust taste with salt and black pepper.

3. Spoon the beef mixture into the baking dish and spread evenly in the dish.

4. Sprinkle with cheese and bake in the oven for 15 minutes until cheese has melted and golden brown.

5. Remove and cool for 4 minutes and serve with low carb crusted bread.

Per serving: Calories 385, Fat 25g, Net Carbs 5g, Protein 20g

Chapter 6: Desserts

Lemon-Yogurt Mousse

Prep + Cook Time: 5 minutes +cooling time | Serves: 4

Ingredients

- 24 oz plain yogurt, strained overnight in a cheesecloth
- 2 cups swerve confectioner's sugar
- 2 lemons, juiced and zested
- Pink salt to taste
- 1 cup whipped cream + extra for garnish

Directions

1. Whip the plain yogurt in a bowl with a hand mixer until light and fluffy. Mix in the sugar, lemon juice, and salt. Fold in the whipped cream to evenly combine.

2. Spoon the mousse into serving cups and refrigerate to thicken for 1 hour. Swirl with extra whipped cream and garnish lightly with lemon zest. Serve immediately.

Per serving: Calories 223, Fat 18g, Net Carbs 3g, Protein 12g

Saffron Coconut Bars

Prep + Cook Time: 3 hours | Serves: 4

Ingredients

- 3 ½ ounces ghee
- 10 saffron threads
- 1 ¼ cups coconut milk
- 1 ¾ cups shredded coconut
- 4 tbsp stevia
- 1 tsp cardamom powder

Directions

1. Combine the shredded coconut with 1 cup of the coconut milk. In another bowl, mix together the remaining coconut milk with the stevia and saffron. Let sit for 30 minutes.

2. Heat the ghee in a wok. Add the coconut mixture as well as the saffron mixture, and cook for 5 minutes on low heat, mixing continuously. Stir in the cardamom and cook for another 5 minutes.

3. Spread the mixture onto a small container and freeze for 2 hours. Cut into bars to serve.

Per serving: Calories 215, Fat: 22g, Net Carbs: 1.4g, Protein: 2g

Peanut Dark Chocolate Barks

Prep + Cook Time: 5 minutes | Serves: 6

Ingredients

- 10 oz unsweetened dark chocolate, chopped
- ½ cup erythritol
- ¼ cup dried cranberries, chopped
- ¼ cup toasted peanuts, chopped
- ¼ tsp salt

Directions

1. Line a baking sheet with parchment paper. Pour chocolate and erythritol in a bowl, and melt in the microwave for 25 seconds, stirring three times until fully melted.

2. Stir in the cranberries, peanuts, and salt, reserving a few cranberries and peanuts for garnishing.

3. Pour the mixture on the baking sheet and spread out. Sprinkle with remaining cranberries and peanuts. Refrigerate for 2 hours to set.

4. Break into bite-size pieces to serve.

Per serving: Calories 225, Fat 21g, Net Carbs 3g, Protein 6g

Coffee Balls

Prep + Cook Time: 3 minutes + cooling time | Serves: 6

Ingredients

- 1 ½ cups mascarpone cheese
- ½ cup melted ghee
- ½ cup melted ghee
- 3 tbsp unsweetened cocoa powder
- ¼ cup erythritol
- 6 tbsp brewed coffee, room temperature

Directions

1. Whisk the mascarpone cheese, ghee, cocoa powder, erythritol, and coffee with a hand mixer until creamy and fluffy, for 1 minute.

2. Fill into muffin tins and freeze for 3 hours until firm.

Per serving: Calories 145, Fat 14g, Net Carbs 2g, Protein 4g

Dark Chocolate Cheesecake Bites

Prep + Cook Time: 4 minutes + cooling time | Serves: 6

Ingredients

- 10 oz unsweetened dark chocolate chips
- ½ half and half
- 20 oz cream cheese, softened
- ½ cup swerve
- 1 tsp vanilla extract

Directions

1. In a saucepan, melt the chocolate with half and a half on low heat for 1 minute. Turn the heat off.

2. In a bowl, whisk the cream cheese, swerve, and vanilla extract with a hand mixer until smooth. Stir into the chocolate mixture. Spoon into silicone muffin tins and freeze for 4 hours until firm.

Per serving: Calories 241, Fat 22g, Net Carbs 3.1g, Protein 5g

Coconut Butter Ice Cream

Prep + Cook Time: 50 minutes + cooling time | Serves: 4

Ingredients

- ½ cup smooth coconut butter
- ½ cup swerve
- 3 cups half and half
- 1 tsp vanilla extract
- 2 pinches salt

Directions

1. Beat coconut butter and swerve in a bowl with a hand mixer until smooth. Gradually whisk in half and half until thoroughly combined.

2. Mix in vanilla and salt. Pour mixture into a loaf pan and freeze for 45 minutes until firmed up. Scoop into glasses when ready to eat and serve.

Per serving: Calories 290, Fat 23g, Net Carbs 6g, Protein 13g

Mom's Walnut Cookies

Prep + Cook Time: 25 minutes | Serves: 12

Ingredients

- 1 egg
- 2 cups ground pecans
- ¼ cup sweetener
- ½ tsp baking soda
- 1 tbsp ghee
- 20 walnuts halves

Directions

1. Preheat the oven to 350°F. Mix the ingredients, except the walnuts, until combined.

2. Make 20 balls out of the mixture and press them with your thumb onto a lined cookie sheet. Top each cookie with a walnut half. Bake for about 12 minutes.

Per serving: Calories 101, Fat: 11g, Net Carbs: 0.6g, Protein: 1.6g

Tasty Hot Chocolate with Peanuts

Prep + Cook Time: 7 minutes | Serves: 4

Ingredients

- 3 cups almond milk
- 4 tbsp unsweetened cocoa powder
- 2 tbsp swerve
- 3 tbsp peanut butter
- Finely chopped peanuts to garnish

Directions

1. In a saucepan, add the almond milk, cocoa powder, and swerve. Stir the mixture until the sugar dissolves. Set the pan over low to heat through for 5 minutes, without boiling.

2. Swirl the mix occasionally. Turn the heat off and stir in the peanut butter to be incorporated. Pour the hot chocolate into mugs and sprinkle with chopped peanuts. Serve warm.

Per serving: Calories 225, Fat 21.5g, Net Carbs 0.6g, Protein 4.5g

Berry, Mascarpone and Pistachio Bowl

Prep + Cook Time: 8 minutes | Serves: 4

Ingredients

- 4 cups Greek yogurt
- liquid stevia to taste
- 1 ½ cups mascarpone cheese
- 1 ½ cups blueberries and raspberries
- 1 cup raw pistachios

Directions

1. Mix the yogurt, stevia, and mascarpone in a bowl until evenly combined. Divide the mixture into 4 bowls, share the berries and pistachios on top of the cream.

2. Serve the dessert immediately.

Per serving: Calories 480, Fat 40g, Net Carbs 5g, Protein 20g

Cardamom Cookies

Prep + Cook Time: 25 minutes | Serves: 4

Ingredients

- 2 cups almond flour
- ½ tsp baking soda
- ¾ cup sweetener
- ½ cup butter, softened
- 1 tbsp vanilla extract

Coating:

- 2 tbsp erythritol sweetener
- 1 tsp ground cardamom

Directions

1. Preheat your oven to 350°F. Combine all cookie ingredients in a bowl. Make 16 balls out of the mixture and flatten them with hands. Combine the cardamom and erythritol. Dip the cookies in the cardamom mixture and arrange them on a lined cookie sheet. Cook for 15 minutes, until crispy.

Per serving: Calories 131, Fat: 13g, Net Carbs: 1.5g, Protein: 3g

Keto Fat Bombs

Prep + Cook Time: 3 minutes + cooling time | Serves: 4

Ingredients

- ½ cup peanut butter
- ½ cup coconut oil
- 4 tbsp unsweetened cocoa powder
- ½ cup erythritol

Directions

1. Melt butter and coconut oil in the microwave for 45 seconds, stirring twice until properly melted and mixed. Mix in cocoa powder and erythritol until completely combined. Pour into muffin moulds and refrigerate for 3 hours to harden.

Per serving: Calories 193, Fat 18.3g, Net Carbs 2g, Protein 4g

The 20-Day Meal Plan To Lose 20 Pounds

Day	Breakfast	Lunch	Dinner	Dessert/ Snacks	Kkal
1	Coconut Almond Muffins	American Cobb Egg Salad in Lettuce Wraps	Prosciutto-Wrapped Chicken with Asparagus	Coconut Butter Ice Cream	1,403
2	Chorizo, Collard Greens and Avocado Eggs	Thyme Tomato Soup	Paleo Coconut Flour Chicken Nuggets	Dark Chocolate Cheesecake Bites (2)	1,483
3	Cauliflower and Ham Baked Eggs	Eggplant Chicken Gratin With Swiss Cheese	Pickled Peppers and Grilled Beef Salad with Feta	Saffron Coconut Bars(2)	1,501
4	Creamy Salmon Tortilla Wraps	Pancetta Wrapped Chicken Rolls	Provolone Chicken Spinach Bake	Coffee Balls (2)	1,503
5	Swiss Cheese Chorizo Waffles	Creamy Chicken Thighs	Turkey with Avocado Sauce	Keto Fat Bombs (2)	1,481
6	Keto Breakfast Beef Stacks with Lemon	Beef Burgers with Roasted Brussels Sprouts	Smothered Chicken Breasts with Bacon	Lemon-Yogurt Mousse	1,479
7	Tofu Scramble with Mushrooms and Spinach	Chicken Breasts with Jarred Pickle Juice	Tomato Basil Stuffed Chicken Breasts	Mom's Walnut Cookies (3)	1,497
8	Cauliflower and Ham Baked Eggs	Grilled BBQ Pork Chops	Cheesy Chicken Tenders	Spicy Smoked Mackerel Cakes	1,538
9	Spinach and Fontina Cheese Nest Bites	Colby Cauliflower Soup with Pancetta Chips	Baked Chicken Skewers with Rutabaga Fries	Tasty Hot Chocolate with Peanuts	1,436
10	Bok Choy Squash Omelet with Sausage	Prawns, Avocado and Cauliflower Salad	Tuna Salad Pickle Boats (2)	Berry, Mascarpone Pistachio Bowl	1,488

11	Frittata with Spinach and Ricotta	Baked Tenderloin with Lime Chimichurri	Grilled Garlic Chicken with Steamed Cauliflower	Chili Baked Zucchini Sticks	1,451
12	Sausage and Grana Padano Egg Muffins	Pancetta Mashed Cauliflower	Paprika Chicken Bacon Stew	Parmesan Green Bean Crisps (2)	1,477
13	Zucchini Quiche with Pancetta Breakfast	Grilled BBQ Pork Chops	Chicken with Tomato and Zucchini	Paprika Dill Deviled Eggs	1,449
14	Cucumber-Turkey Canapes (2)	Baked Pulled Pork Tenderloin with Avocado	Cheese Muffins with Ajillo Mushrooms	Dark Chocolate Cheesecake Bites	1411
15	Cream Cheese and Turkey Tortilla Rolls	Beef Stir-Fry with Peanut Sauce	Roasted Chicken with Yogurt Scallions Sauce	Lemon-Yogurt Mousse (2)	1,519
16	Sausage and Grana Padano Egg Muffins	Fish Taco Bowl with Broccoli, Avocado and Cabbage	Beef with Broccoli Rice and Eggs	Berry, Mascarpone Pistachio Bowl	1,492
17	Tofu Scramble with Mushrooms and Spinach	Colby Cauliflower Soup with Pancetta Chips	Polish Beef Tripe	Keto Fat Bombs (2)	1,406
18	Coconut Almond Muffins	Eggplant Chicken Gratin With Swiss Cheese	Beef Broccoli Curry	Cardamom Cookies (3)	1,499
19	Chorizo, Collard Greens and Avocado Eggs	Gourmet Caesar Salad with Poached Eggs and Smoked Salmon	Spinach Cheese Stuffed Flank Steak Rolls	Rosemary Cheese Chips with Guacamole (2)	1,482
20	Spinach and Fontina Cheese Nest Bites	Beef Burgers with Roasted Brussels Sprouts	Baked Stuffed Avocados	Cream Cheese and Turkey Tortilla Rolls (2)	1,547

Printed in Great Britain
by Amazon